African American Atheists and Political Liberation

The History of African American Religions

UNIVERSITY PRESS OF FLORIDA

Florida A&M University, Tallahassee
Florida Atlantic University, Boca Raton
Florida Gulf Coast University, Ft. Myers
Florida International University, Miami
Florida State University, Tallahassee
University of Central Florida, Orlando
University of Florida, Gainesville
University of North Florida, Jacksonville
University of South Florida, Tampa
University of West Florida, Pensacola

THE HISTORY OF AFRICAN-AMERICAN RELIGIONS
Edited by Stephen W. Angell and Anthony Pinn

Laborers in the Vineyard of the Lord: The Beginnings of the AME Church in Florida, 1865–1895, by Larry Eugene Rivers and Canter Brown, Jr. (2001)

Between Cross and Crescent: Christian and Muslim Perspectives on Malcolm and Martin, by Lewis V. Baldwin and Amiri YaSin Al-Hadid (2002)

The Quest for the Cuban Christ: A Historical Search, by Miguel A. De La Torre (2002)

For a Great and Grand Purpose: The Beginnings of the AMEZ Church in Florida, 1864–1905, by Canter Brown, Jr., and Larry Eugene Rivers (2004)

Afro-Cuban Religiosity, Revolution, and National Identity, by Christine Ayorinde (2004)

From Garvey to Marley: Rastafari Theology, by Noel Leo Erskine (2005)

Hell Without Fires: Slavery, Christianity & the Antebellum Spiritual Narrative, by Yolanda Pierce (2005)

Where Men Are Wives and Mothers Rule: Santería Ritual Practices and Their Gender Implications, by Mary Ann Clark (2005)

Around the Family Altar: Domesticity in the African Methodist Episcopal Church, 1865–1900, by Julius H. Bailey (2005)

Black Blood Brothers: Confraternities and Social Mobility for Africans and Their Descendants in New Spain, by Nicole von Germeten (2006)

African American Atheists and Political Liberation: A Study of the Sociocultural Dynamics of Faith, by Michael Lackey (2007)

African American Atheists and Political Liberation

A STUDY OF THE SOCIOCULTURAL DYNAMICS OF FAITH

Michael Lackey

University Press of Florida

Gainesville Tallahassee Tampa Boca Raton
Pensacola Orlando Miami Jacksonville Ft. Myers

12 11 10 09 08 07   6 5 4 3 2 1

Library of Congress Cataloging-in-Publication Data:
Lackey, Michael.
African American atheists and political liberation : a study of the sociocultural
dynamics of faith / Michael Lackey.
p. cm.
Includes bibliographical references and index.
ISBN-13: 978-0-8130-3035-7 (alk. paper)
1. American literature—African American authors—History and criticism.
2. Atheism and literature—United States—History—20th century. 3. African
Americans in literature. 4. African Americans—Religion—History—20th
century. 5. African American authors—Political and social views. 6. Wright,
Richard, 1908–1960—Criticism and interpretation. 7. Larsen, Nella—Criticism
and interpretation. 8. Hughes, Langston, 1902–1967—Criticism and interpretation.
I. Title.
PS153.N5.L33 2007
810.9'8960739–dc22   2006022841

Excerpts from *Dust Tracks on a Road* by Zora Neale Hurston. Copyright 1942
by Zora Neale Hurston; renewed copyright 1970 by John C. Hurston. Reprinted
by permission of HarperCollins Publishers.

Excerpts from *The Outsider* by Richard Wright. Copyright 1953 by Richard
Wright; renewed copyright 1981 by Ellen Wright. Reprinted by permission of
HarperCollins Publishers.

Excerpt from *Short Stories* by Langston Hughes. Copyright 1996 by Ramona Bass
and Arnold Rampersad. Reprinted by permission of Hill and Wang, a division of
Farrar, Straus and Giroux, LLC.

The University Press of Florida is the scholarly publishing agency for the State
University System of Florida, comprising Florida A&M University, Florida
Atlantic University, Florida Gulf Coast University, Florida International
University, Florida State University, University of Central Florida, University
of Florida, University of North Florida, University of South Florida, and
University of West Florida.

University Press of Florida
15 Northwest 15th Street
Gainesville, FL 32611-2079
http://www.upf.com

For Julie, Anya, and Katya

Contents

Acknowledgments

Over the years, many have helped me formulate the ideas in this book, too many to name in this short acknowledgments page. But I would like to mention just a few of the major players in my life. I owe a great debt to John Wright for introducing me to the Harlem Renaissance. Over the years, Tony Pinn has encouraged me to pursue this project, even as he challenged many of my conclusions. Without Tony's valuable insight and his unflagging support, I could not have written this book. I am grateful to Charles Long for his discerning remarks about my work on Fanon. His input has enabled me to articulate my arguments more clearly and forcefully. I thank James A. Miller for helping me to clarify my thinking about Richard Wright, and I owe much to Dana Nelson and Norm Allen for their astute comments on a draft of this book.

I would like to express my gratitude to the Alexander von Humboldt Foundation, which provided a generous fellowship that allowed me to do much of the research for this project. I would also like to thank Ludwig Pfeiffer, my German sponsor, who always challenged me to be more accurate and precise. I thank SUNY–Brockport for a faculty award that provided funding for my excellent research assistant, Michael Herman, and I thank Wellesley College for a faculty grant that provided funding for my very capable student worker, Siena Napoleon-Bruno.

Finally, I would like to thank my wife, Julie Eckerle, for her loving support. I only hope that I can inspire and support her work as much as she inspires and supports mine.

Introduction

African American Atheism

A Cause for Hope

"I simply rejected religion. I rejected God. Not my instincts, but my deepest feelings revolted compulsively—not because I was I, a sort of neutral human stuff reacting directly to experience, but because I was a Negro."

J. Saunders Redding, *On Being Negro in America*

This book contains uncharitable observations about belief in God and religious communities. The atheists in this study do not mourn the retreating sea of faith (Matthew Arnold's *Dover Beach*), nor do they consider a godless world just a heap of broken images (T. S. Eliot's *The Waste Land*). On the topics of God and religion, they are blasphemous, unkind, and relentless. The tone in their writing is mocking, irreverent, and flippant, and their judgments are decisive. Instead of finding hope and love through belief in God, the African American atheists in this book claim that "God and the word of God have been used to perpetuate the wicked idea of human inferiority" (Redding 147). Indeed, for the writers in this study, since God is primarily a weapon that can be used to oppress and violate culturally designated inferiors with impunity, they consider the leap of faith an unethical act of the intellect.

This is not to say that the writers in this study consider the God concept an inherently evil idea, which leads necessarily to crimes against humanity. Rather, they consider the God concept an empty signifier, a semiotic vacuity that political powers can easily control and exploit in order to construct and sanction an oppressive politics, to mobilize the necessary forces to disseminate and legislate an unjust legal system, and to conceal atrocities from both themselves and their victims. Abolishing the God concept would certainly not eliminate a politics of oppression, they would argue, but it would divest the dominant power of its most effective weapon for enacting its political agenda and for interpellating the masses, those individuals who must accept the system with their whole heart, their whole soul, and their whole mind for it to function. For the African American atheists in this study, killing God would be the first step toward the construction of a truly tolerant and egalitarian democracy.

There is not only value in but also a profound need for a sustained study of African American atheism. While there have been some excellent books on atheism in the last forty-five years, like J. Hillis Miller's *The Disappearance of God*, John Towner Frederick's *The Darkened Sky*, Susan E. Lorsch's *Where Nature Ends*, Alfred Kazin's *God and the American Writer*, and A. N. Wilson's *God's Funeral*, these studies do not address the rich contributions of African American atheists. As a consequence, these studies, focusing as they do on writers like Matthew Arnold, Robert Browning, Thomas Hardy, Herman Melville, Joseph Conrad, and Robert Frost, tend to frame the questions and issues regarding God's death in a way that radically differs from black atheists. Moreover, this intellectual orientation leads to an emotional response that is the exact opposite of those in the African American tradition. Consider, for instance, this passage from Jean-Paul Sartre, an atheist who articulates the seemingly dominant response to God's death: "The existentialist . . . thinks it very distressing that God does not exist, because all possibility of finding values in a heaven of ideas disappears along with Him; there can no longer be an *a priori* Good, since there is no infinite and perfect consciousness to think it" (Sartre 40–41). From this atheistic perspective, God legitimizes authentic knowledge, which can be used to establish a well-grounded moral system. God's death, therefore, means the loss of not only true knowledge but also a moral universe, which is why such atheists fall prey to melancholic mourning.[1] Indeed, on discovering that there can be neither a priori knowledge nor a metaphysics of morals, atheists in this tradition languish over humanity's "radical sense of inner nothingness" (Miller 8) or how "we live in an empty, Godless universe, devoid of purpose" (Wilson 25). Foundational to the despairing atheists' emotional orientation toward life is a philosophical yearning for certain Knowledge or an objective Truth, a yearning that is thwarted by God's exit from the universe.

Since God has so very often been used as a weapon against black people, atheist writers of African descent reject the idea of certain or objective Knowledge as an absurd proposition. As Frantz Fanon observes, if God is the basis and foundation for objective knowledge, then such knowledge has consistently had very non-objective consequences, for "objectivity is always directed against" the culturally designated inferior (*Wretched* 77). In very specific terms, "God made" white people "to rule over the lower breeds" (Wright, *Outsider* 264). This usage of the God concept was not uncommon, as I will demonstrate throughout this book. Therefore, it should come as no surprise that for African American atheists, who have witnessed how the God concept has been used to justify the biological and intellectual inferiority of people of African descent, God's death does not lead to existential despair. On the contrary, for African American atheists, atheism is cause for rejoicing, since it effectively divests the dominant political powers of their most powerful weapon against culturally designated inferiors.

Therefore, instead of asking questions about the nature of knowledge and morality in a theistic or post-theistic world, African American atheists ask: If the God concept plays a role in the formation of a legal or political system, who will reap the benefits? Who will suffer the consequences? What role does the God concept play in the formation of psychological and cultural habits of mind? How does it determine interactions between various races? How does the God concept function in determining the relationship of a superpower to a vulnerable foreign Other? Such questions are less concerned with the nature of God, which is an incoherent idea for African American atheists, than they are with the pragmatic and political functions of the God concept.

It is this political focus on the God concept that separates my work from someone like Paul Tillich's, whose *Dynamics of Faith* is the basis for the subtitle of this book. Tillich realizes that faith and the God concept have been used to justify horrendous crimes against humanity, but such crimes, he argues, were the product of false understandings of religion or a perverted version of faith. Were the culture to embrace "genuine religion," which is grounded on a proper understanding of the dynamics of faith, then such crimes would not be so prevalent.[2] No doubt, Tillich's view of faith and religion is profoundly humane, one based on principles of tolerance, inclusion, and respect. And yet, from the perspective of the atheists in this study, his claim to have epistemological access to such a thing as "genuine religion" or the essence of faith is the basis and foundation of a politics of oppression.

At issue here are two opposing theories of knowledge, one that presupposes the existence of mind-independent Concepts (concepts that would exist even if there were no humans and therefore must be discovered), which only full-fledged Humans humans are epistemologically stationed to know, and one that treats knowledge as a psychosemiotic construction, a view in which "concepts" are psychological projections that assume a provisional form in and through a semiotic sign. According to the first theory of knowledge, there are such things as a true Morality, a true Religion, a true God-Concept, true Faith, etc., and if some people fail to know and understand such true Concepts, they are either evil or not fully realized Humans. The second theory of "knowledge" considers concepts extremely valuable but albeit provisional "forms" of meaning that shift in relation to the ever-changing resources, needs, and desires of various language communities. The idea that there is such a thing as true Religion, true Morality, or true Faith is simply incomprehensible to those who subscribe to this second theory of "knowledge." Although thinkers in this tradition do not believe that concepts are mind-independent or universally valid, it does not follow that they consider language and knowledge useless and/or invalid. They just consider "knowledge" limited by virtue of its creators' limitations, in need of perpetual transformation to keep pace with the emerging interests and desires of language users, and subject to endless negotiations with and among the competing producers of "knowledge." But most important, those who subscribe to this second theory of "knowledge" believe that, by rejecting the first theory of Knowledge, they have overcome the single most dehumanizing weapon that theists have wielded in order to dominate, control, and violate culturally designated inferiors with impunity. Authentic Knowledge, that is, Knowledge of the true Anything, whether it is religion, God, or morality, has been the basis for determining and subsequently stratifying humanness. Those who have epistemological access to true Religion, true Morality, or true Truth are full-fledged Humans, while those who lack such Knowledge are subhuman or nonhuman. In short, the theory of objective Knowledge has been used to determine humanness. But if we all agree that "knowledge" is nothing more than psychosemiotic construction, then it would be impossible to use knowledge as a means of determining who is fully human and who is not.

Therefore, within the context of this book, the most important issue is the African American atheists' examination of the role that the God concept has played in determining humanness and, by implication, defining certain others as sub- or nonhuman. To be sure, the claim that people of African descent were considered and treated as animals is common knowledge in the critical discourses of our day, but there has been a scholarly resistance to examine precisely the extent to which the God concept and/or a spiritual mentality is the basis and foundation for a systematic theory and a practical politics of dehumanization. For the writers discussed in this book, however, the God concept or a spiritual concept is the necessary intellectual and political point of departure for grounding an oppressive sociopolitical system. But it is not enough to simply claim that the God concept was used to justify treating mi-norities like animals ("lower breeds") or as an "ape made by God to cut wood and draw water." What is needed is a detailed explanation of the intricate ways that God-based systems of knowledge and subjectivity have functioned to stratify humanness and subhumanness and to make such a stratification so natural that questioning or challenging it would not even be considered a possibility.

That earlier scholars of atheism have not examined this idea does not in-validate their major conclusions. The studies of Hillis Miller, Lorsch, and Kazin are extremely provocative and valuable, and my own take on atheism owes much to their pioneering efforts. Furthermore, this book would not be possible without the scholarship of Benjamin E. Mays, Norm Allen, William R. Jones, and Anthony B. Pinn, who have done the groundbreaking work of identifying, anthologizing, and interpreting the work of African American atheists and humanists. But the recent work on queer theory, postcolonialism, feminism, cultural criticism, and deconstruction has provided us with new models for examining and interpreting literary texts, cultural movements, and the religious mentality, and since my work makes use of insights and methods from each one of these theoretical approaches, I shed different light on the African American atheist's critique of faith.

Let me briefly indicate how my work differs from earlier studies. In the introduction to *By These Hands*, Pinn notes that, while many consider the United States a country "founded upon overtly religious ideals and desires," there was from the country's inception systemic abuse of "Native Americans, African Americans, women, and powerless Europeans." Such treatment, Pinn claims, suggests that the religious majority in America was out of step with "the basic principles of the Christian faith" (1). This has been the standard in-terpretive approach to the Christian abuse of the culturally designated inferior or to the Christian justification of atrocities. Christianity embodies the ideals of justice, fairness, and righteousness. Therefore, if people commit crimes of any sort against others, their behavior contradicts "the basic principles of the Christian faith."

In the excellent study *Canaan Land*, Albert J. Raboteau uses this approach to analyze the Christian's justification of slavery in the United States. After discussing how African Americans identified with the plight of the Ancient Hebrews in Egypt, he argues that the biblical story of Exodus embodies the true meaning of the faith, and therefore "[t]he story of Exodus contradict-ed the claim made by defenders of slavery that God intended Africans to be slaves. On the contrary, Exodus proved that slavery was against God's will and that slavery would end someday" (44). In his brilliantly researched book *The Arrogance of Faith*, Forrest G. Wood impressively documents how "Christian thought and conduct in the first three centuries of American life came down overwhelmingly on the side of human oppression" (36). But for Wood, the early American Christian's oppressive behavior is an irreconcilable "contradiction" of the Christian faith, which exalts "peace on earth and good will toward men" (37). Therefore, instead of tracing the American Christian's oppressive behavior back to a Christian source or the Christian mentality, Wood faults racism, which "subverted the best of principles."

For the atheists in this study, the distinction between an oppressive Christianity and a pure ideal is simply untenable, because atheism effectively abolishes the idea of a mind-independent Concept (the unadulterated ideal), which is what it is whether humans perceive it or not. To put this in the words of Jacques Derrida: "To write is to know that what has not yet been produced within literality has no other dwelling place, does not await us as prescription in some *topos ouranios*, or some divine understanding. Meaning must await being said or written in order to inhabit itself and in order to become, by differing from itself, what it is: meaning" ("Force" 11). Concepts, knowledge, and meaning are not pre-given entities created by God and waiting to be plucked out of some *topos ouranios*; they are human constructions that will always reflect the biases and ideology of their human creators. Richard Rorty articulates this distinctly atheistic view of knowledge and meaning when he indicates how God's death rendered essentialist discourses about the human or the world meaningless and incoherent: "The very idea that the world or the self has an intrinsic nature—one which the physicist or the poet may have glimpsed—is a remnant of the idea that the world is a divine creation, the work of someone who had something in mind, who Himself spoke some language in which He described His own project" (21). Distinctive to this atheistic view is the rejection of a transcendental signifier that could be used to identify conceptual perversions. Put more concretely, for Pinn, Raboteau, and Wood to suggest that the oppressive behavior of Christians contradicts the pure and true religion of Christianity, they would have to appeal to some sort of transcendental signifier (the pure ideal Christianity that would never sanction oppression). But for the atheists in this study, there are no pure ideals independent of the human mind.

At this point, let me qualify the atheists' claim about religious essentialism. Atheists do not object to religion and the God concept because they consist of specific precepts that lead necessarily to crimes against humanity. After all, religions and believers contradict each other regularly on every point of faith, morality, ethics, and politics. What troubles atheists so much is what I refer to as religion's contentless essentialism. Whether it is a southern statesman of the early nineteenth century who sees in the Bible justification for slavery or a Quaker abolitionist who sees in the life of Christ a model for liberation, the argument that believers of every stripe consistently make is that they have epistemological access to the true faith and that people who hold a contradictory belief have a perverted or distorted view of religion and/or God. For atheists, therefore, religion is contentless, because it has justified and can justify anything and everything, from polygamy to monogamy, from subjugating women to liberating women, from genocide to pacifism, and from rabid capitalism to monastic poverty. But it is also essentializing, because whatever truth the practitioners accept is considered the true faith, while those who contradict the true faith are treated as if their faith were a perversion or distortion of the true faith.

For atheists, it is this essentializing tendency that has enabled religious people to identify and define certain groups of people as culturally designated inferiors and then to justify violating and abusing them.[3] Anti- and postcolonial theorists have done the best work detailing the way the religious mentality has justified such violations and abuse. For instance, anti-imperialists like R. B. Cunninghame Graham, E. M. Forster, Aimé Césaire, and Frantz Fanon have examined how the religious view of the Chosen People has justified and even necessitated the subjugation and domination of the non-chosen. What makes individuals Chosen People is their epistemological capacity to know God and His Truths. Given this epistemological capacity, believers have access to a transcendental signifier like the pure ideal of Christianity, and on the basis of their capacity to have such Knowledge, they qualify as people in the strict sense of the word. In short, Knowledge of a transcendental signifier makes a person fully human, so if certain individuals lack such Knowledge, we can assume that they are not fully human. Therefore, the Chosen People can rule and govern the non-chosen, and should they reject or threaten the Chosen People's authority, the Chosen have the right and even the obligation to kill them.

In an anti-imperialist lecture delivered to the Weybridge Literary Society in 1909, the British novelist, E.M. Forster sheds some light on this Chosen People mentality when he notes how the non-chosen are treated "as a sort of moral football, designed by providence for the purpose of keeping the Chosen

Race in good condition. Smash 'em up. Smash up the Gentiles. They're sure to be plotting against us, if only we could understand their beastly lingo. Teach them that we are the chosen race and that they aren't, that we have the Law and they haven't, that we are the real Jungle Folk and they the gibbering monkeys."[4] Atheists in the postcolonial tradition do not just reject the idea of a transcendental signifier because it is a dubious and untenable concept; they reject it because it is the basis and foundation for stratifying humanness ("we are the chosen race and they are not") and thereby for justifying violence and abuse against those who do not qualify as human ("gibbering monkeys") in the strict sense of the word.

My use of Derrida, Rorty, Forster, and Fanon in a book about African American atheism should immediately give my reader pause. A white French poststructuralist, a white liberal pragmatist, a white British novelist, and a French-Martinican psychiatrist—why are these individuals significant in a study about African American atheism? African American religious scholar William R. Jones will help me justify the inclusion of so many seemingly tangential figures (and there are many more such references throughout the book). Jones rightly claims that many African American atheists "trace their [intellectual] lineage to the enlightenment or the scientific revolution," but he also cautions scholars to note that African Americans, in formulating their critique of the God concept, develop their criticisms "from radically different socio-economic contexts" than traditional Enlightenment rationalists, and as a consequence, "the question of God [for African Americans] is posed in different ways" (42).

In doing a study of African American atheism, there is a twofold interpretive danger. As any scholar familiar with the work of prominent twentieth-century African American writers knows, such writers were well versed in intellectual history and conversant in the major intellectual debates of their day. Few intellectuals could ever compare with W.E.B. DuBois or Alain Locke. While it is possible to read a Richard Wright novel without knowing Martin Heidegger's "Letter on Humanism" or Jean-Paul Sartre's *Being and Nothingness*, an understanding of the issues and assumptions implicit in these works sheds considerable light on *The Outsider*. Therefore, to understand the work of such prominent African American atheists, it is extremely useful to outline the traditions to which they were appealing and the intellectual developments their work anticipated.

But it is equally important not to see their work as merely derivative. Given the way white European and American scholars and writers have contributed to a culture of oppression and domination (something that Edward Said so brilliantly documents in his masterpiece *Culture and Imperialism* and Charles W. Mills clarifies in his excellent study *The Racial Contract*), it would be naïve to think that brilliant writers and thinkers like Nella Larsen, Langston Hughes, and Zora Neale Hurston would simply accept the standard white version of the history of ideas or the philosophical conclusions of a contemporary debate. As John Ernest claims, in producing their own intellectual sense of their communal selves, "African Americans necessarily had to contend with and against the developing tradition of white American historical thought as well as the pointed erasure of Africa as a site of history and Enlightenment thought" (5). Put differently, the writers I discuss in *African American Atheists and Political Liberation*, while conversant in the theories and philosophies of their day and the traditions of which they were a part, were also charting new ways of thinking about the issues, drawing new lines of connection between ideas, and arriving at sometimes slightly, sometimes radically different conclusions. Therefore, in my analysis, I place each writer within a larger intellectual context in order to understand the religious and atheistic issues at stake, but I ultimately focus on the African American atheists' particular critique of the sociocultural dynamics of faith. It is my contention that African American atheists were best able to shed the most light on the political function of the God concept to sanction overt and covert forms of violence and abuse. In short, it is important, as Jones claims, to locate these writers within their respective intellectual traditions, but it is also important to note how these writers specifically rework these traditions in light of their own unique experience of the world. Therefore, in my analysis of the writers in this book, I draw from a variety of writers and traditions, but my ultimate objective is to indicate how and why the African American atheist tradition has been so effective in shedding most light on the destructive sociocultural dynamics of faith. Indeed, if my findings prove convincing, I suspect that we can use the insights of African American atheists to detail precisely how the religious mind-set has been used to violate so many groups, like women, gays, lesbians, atheists, agnostics, the poor, non-Christians, non-Moslems, non-Jews, unwed mothers, interracial couples, etc.

There is another reason for my seemingly scattered references throughout this book. As a scholar, I find the concept of ideology to be the most important contribution to the history of ideas in the last two hundred years. While I could invoke Karl Marx, Raymond Williams, Louis Althusser, Michel Foucault, Judith Butler, or Stuart Hall to define ideology at this point, I prefer Friedrich Nietzsche, whose formulation best clarifies why I approach my subject matter as I do. In *The Case of Wagner*, Nietzsche claims: "But all of us have, unconsciously, involuntarily in our bodies values, words, formulas, moralities of *opposite* descent—we are, physiologically considered, *false*" (192). For Nietzsche, the beginning of "knowledge" is to recognize our physiologically false condition. Since we have been claimed at the level of the unconscious by our culture's "values, words, formulas, [and] moralities," we can never be physiologically true.[5] But we can be less false if we understand that we have been possessed at the level of the unconscious. Only when we acknowledge that our conscious and rational systems of knowledge have been, in large measure, predetermined by the unconscious knowledge (what some scholars have dubbed ideology) that inhabits our bodies can we begin to have a clearer understanding of our physiologically false condition. In other words, what Nietzsche suggests is that we can, through a careful analysis of the ideologies that inhabit our bodies at an unconscious level, achieve some level of authenticity and have some genuine insight into ourselves and our culture. But because the ideologies that inhabit our bodies are, for the most part, unconscious, we will never have a comprehensive understanding of ourselves or our culture.

Such a recognition of the unconscious nature of ideology necessitates intellectual blind spots, so when a great writer and thinker like Richard Wright examines the destructive sociocultural consequences of the religious mindset, he is likely to see some things with stunning clarity and to miss others altogether. Put more concretely, while Wright brilliantly exposes how the God concept is used by whites to ontologize nonwhites as "half-human" and "lower breeds," he never really examines how it is frequently used by men to ontologize women as subhuman. But Nella Larsen certainly understands exactly how the God concept has effectively divested women of power and authority over their own bodies. And yet, despite Larsen's brilliant insight, she does not really address how the God concept functions ideologically in relation to the body politic or the legal system. Langston Hughes, however, understands all too well how the political and legal systems work in tandem with the culture's religious mind-set to disenfranchise and dehumanize black people. In short, each one of these writers is astutely aware of the dangerous and destructive consequences of the God concept within a particular framework, but each is limited by virtue of his or her own ideological orientation and subsequent blind spots. When organizing the material in this book, therefore, my objective has been to play to each writer's strengths: Redding's and Wright's philosophical orientation, Larsen's feminist focus, Hughes's concern with the legal system, and Hurston's biblical expertise.

Put simply, my approach is driven by my commitment to the methodology of cultural studies, which, to my mind, Rita Felski defines most clearly and intelligently: "Cultural studies seeks to detotalize the social field and hence rejects the assumption that any individual work can represent that field. The political pulse of a culture is not to be found in the depths of a single work but rather in a mobile and discontinuous constellation of texts as they play off, influence, and contradict each other. Rather than reading *into* texts, cultural studies seeks to read *across* texts" (512). While I do think, contra Felski, that we can use a single work to take the political pulse of *one part* of the culture, I favor the cultural studies approach of reading across multiple texts to get a more comprehensive view of the culture. Within the context of this book, I think that each one of the writers I have selected has something extremely insightful to say about the distinctive way the God concept has functioned to justify subjugation, dehumanization, violation, and even murder, but I do not think that any single writer or text has or could have clearly articulated in a comprehensive manner how the God concept has functioned to degrade culturally designated inferiors. There are just too many ideological blind spots to have such a comprehensive view. Therefore, the critique in this book is to be found in the communal formulation of the writers I have selected. This is not to say that my book should be considered comprehensive or complete, for I am certain that I have many ideological blind spots. But if my intuition is right, that there exists an extremely vibrant community of African American atheists that has detailed with stunning precision the way the God concept consistently justifies overt and covert acts of physical and psychological violence against culturally designated inferiors, then one could see this book as merely initiating a dialogue.

Put simply, my objective is to articulate what African American atheists thought about the God concept and why they thought what they thought. But if I did an extended analysis of Lorraine Hansberry's *A Raisin in the Sun*, Toni Morrison's *The Bluest Eye*, or James Baldwin's *The Fire Next Time*, the comprehensive view of this book would look be very different. My hope is that this book will initiate more studies on the topic of African American atheism and the African American atheist's specific critique of the God concept, even if those studies totally reject everything I have tried to accomplish in this study, for it is only in the intense interrogation and discussion of complex and uncomfortable ideas that we will arrive at some genuine insight into the atheistic and religious structures of mind, specifically insofar as those structures play themselves out in the culture at large.

At this point, let me briefly explain how I have structured the argument of *African American Atheists and Political Liberation* chapter by chapter. In the first chapter, I develop the theoretical foundation of the book, a theory that I refer to as an epistemological/ontological recursive loop. Believers have access to a body of knowledge that exceeds the infidel's epistemological reach. For this reason, the infidel will look but not see, listen but not hear, whereas believers will see and hear. On the basis of their epistemological superiority, believers can ontologize the world and others as they will. Specifically, believers are God's chosen, whereas infidels are not. How do we know this? First, because believers can see what the infidel cannot, we can infer that they are epistemologically chosen. Second, given their epistemological superiority, believers can claim that God has told them that they are chosen. Of course, infidels can neither question nor challenge the believers' claims, for they do not possess the believers' privileged epistemology. It is my contention that both Fanon and Redding recognize how the leap of faith establishes this unassailable conceptual system. In other words, both writers understand that it is the religious epistemology that makes the mismeasure of certain groups of people possible. Indeed, both detail how the religious epistemology is used to ontologize certain figures within the culture as "human" and others as "animal" or not human.

Given the believers' epistemological superiority, they not only determine what constitutes the human but, they also have the political and personal freedom to act like a human. In the Judeo-Christian tradition, humans are spiritual beings who, given their spiritual faculty of perception, can know a spiritual truth and conform their lives to that truth. Because people of African descent have been said to lack the ability to access spiritual truth, they would behave like animals, if left to their own resources. For this reason, white believers must instruct and guide the African in the righteous ways of morality. But let us say, just for the sake of argument, that white believers decided to grant that all people are human in the strict sense of the word. Such a declaration, Fanon and Redding would argue, would do nothing to alter the African's dehumanization. The white believer, by conferring personhood on the African, is behaving like a human, a rational being with individual and political agency, whereas the African, though dubbed human, is denied the freedom to act human—he or she is not behaving like an independent agent who has the freedom to constitute "self" as human. It is not enough to be dubbed human; one must have the political freedom to perform the activity that makes one human.

For Fanon and Redding, therefore, to become human, those of African descent must take their humanity. Significantly, this taking presupposes an atheistic orientation toward knowledge and language. The believer claims that he or she can determine personhood through his or her faith-based epistemology. The atheist, however, does not think that the believer has privileged epistemological access to a God-created Truth. Rather, the atheist (from Feuerbach, through Nietzsche and Sartre, to Wright, Fanon, and Redding) claims that knowledge is psychosemiotic projection within a political context. Therefore, becoming human means having the political freedom to name and define oneself, the liberty and ability to construct oneself as human. But to psychosemiotically project self into being as human, it is socially and politically necessary to kill God, for it is the God concept that enables those in power not just to control concepts like the human but also to prevent certain groups from having the political freedom to act like a human.

In the second chapter, I examine a tension in the writings of atheists and humanists. Humanists, who consider humans the arbiters of their own destiny, reject the appeal to the supernatural to ground knowledge of the human. Instead of relying on theological systems to define the human, they acknowledge that it is humans who determine humanness. Not surprisingly, humanists frequently retain the idea of human nature, although their concept is certainly much more inclusive than prehumanist traditions. There is a school of atheists, however, that shares most of the humanists' core values (civil liberties, tolerance, freedom, secular happiness, economic equality, and cultural and intellectual progress), but that resists the idea of human nature. As Jean-Paul Sartre claims in his essay, "The Humanism of Existentialism," "there is no human nature, since there is no God to conceive it" (36).

Richard Wright, who was a friend of Sartre's, certainly understood this radical atheistic view regarding the "human." In fact, this humanist/atheist tension takes center stage in his novel *The Outsider*. While Wright sympathized with the humanistic impulse to treat all humans as human irrespective of race and nation, he was also aware of the potential inconsistencies and dangers implicit in the humanist position. It is my contention that we can best understand Wright's distinctive post-God political vision in *The Outsider*, not by adopting either a strictly humanist or a strictly posthuman interpretation, but by examining the work in light of the tension between humanism and posthumanism. Specifically, the tension between these two traditions provides a basis for understanding the humanistic and atheistic impulse to critique faith systems, to secularize culture, and to formulate a post-God vision of social justice. In other words, we can best understand Cross Damon's critique and rejection of the God concept through the atheist/humanist debate regarding the human.

The third chapter features the most shocking treatment of God and religion in this book. In her novella *Quicksand*, Nella Larsen likens the community of believers to a band of gang rapists. On the surface, such a view of theists is not too terribly offensive, for there has been a tradition of treating God as rapist. In Jeremiah, for instance, Yahweh not only seduces (*patah*) but also rapes (*chasack*) the unwilling prophet. Such a view of God as rapist has inspired writers as varied as John Donne, Teresa of Avila, and Thérèse of Lisieux to use this rape trope in order to highlight their rebellious natures and God's need to use violence to enforce compliance. At issue here is knowledge of a person's fundamental nature and deepest desires. For the believer, union with God is the primary objective of life. Following this logic, when rebellious individuals say no to God, they are acting contrary to their true nature, a nature that believers know and understand. Believers, therefore, interpret no as really meaning yes, which is why they feel justified in imposing their system of belief on the infidel. But for the atheist, since there is no God, the believers' rapelike behavior is not an attempt to bring the apostate back into the fold, but a justification for violating the infidel with impunity. In *Quicksand*, Larsen depicts the main character's conversion, which significantly occurs during a prayer meeting, as a gang rape. After her conversion, Helga is trained to accept on faith that humans have a distinct nature and that preachers have epistemological access to that nature, and should she question or challenge the preacher's construction of reality, the community of believers has at its disposal sophisticated methods to enforce belief. By the end of the novella, however, Helga becomes a militant atheist, an experience that enables her to expose the violent psychology (a metaphorical rape scene) that believers use to entrap people (specifically Helga) into their system. Once she makes this discovery, she then reflects on the way the God concept has been used to violate African Americans en masse.

In the fourth chapter, I examine Hughes's insightful critique of the God concept as it functions in the construction of desire and the Law. As Jacques Derrida and Drucilla Cornell have argued, there is, at a psychological level, an originary violence that structures subjects as desiring beings. This violence is the basis and foundation for establishing an individual and communal orientation toward laws and the Law. But for Hughes, it is the God concept that best functions to persuade culturally marginalized people to internalize laws that ultimately dehumanize and degrade them. Throughout his corpus, Hughes treats the God concept as an empty signifier (a puppet, as he suggests in his poem "Gods"), a semiotic vacuity that political powers can deploy to sanction an oppressive political system. In this chapter, while I allude to a number of Hughes's short stories and poems (like "Father and Son," "Professor," "The Young Glory of Him," and "Goodbye Christ"), I focus my analysis on "Trouble with the Angels." In this story, one of the main characters, Johnny Logan, opposes an unnamed actor who plays the role of God in an all-black play. God has the power to persuade fellow African Americans not only to dance "properly to the tune of Jim Crow" ("Professor") but also to feel that doing so is right and just. Only Johnny is willing to challenge God's authority. But at the end of the story, Johnny, at the behest of God, is arrested and carted off to jail. As he leaves, Johnny is crying. The story concludes with Johnny's fellow actors, who "*wanted* to think Logan was crying because he was being arrested—but in their souls they knew that was not why he wept" (Hughes's emphasis). Through my analysis, I argue that Logan weeps because he understands that the God concept has ultimately gained emotional and therefore legal ascendancy within the bodies and minds of the black community. Consequently, African Americans are extremely vulnerable to being constructed as culturally designated inferiors, which is what Johnny and his fellow actors subconsciously realize. And it is this realization, I argue, that is the real cause of Johnny's tears.

In the fifth chapter, I focus on what I refer to as a Touchstone narrative, which is the atheist's response to the traditional conversion narrative. Traditional conversion narratives generally consist of three stages. In the first, writers express how meaningless and empty their lives were without God. The second stage features their conversion, which occurs either through contact with a community of believers or via a direct experience with "God." The third stage of the narrative is evangelical in nature. The implicit argument runs like this: now that I know God, I am happy and my life is meaningful. If you, dear reader, wish to experience a peace that passes all understanding, then you should take the leap of faith as well.

Touchstone narratives, by contrast, consist of four stages. First, the writer confesses unbelief. Next, the writer has an extremely unpleasant experience with a community of believers. Third, the writer makes an emphatic declaration of unbelief. In the final stage, which is the most important, the writer interrogates the sociocultural consequences of religious belief. Consistent in the Touchstone narratives in this book is the claim that the God concept is personally debilitating and culturally destructive. In this new genre of writing, black atheists produce some of the most insightful analyses of the oppressive sociopolitical functions of the God concept. Indeed, it is my argument that the black atheists' critique of faith will force us to rethink and reconsider earlier studies of atheism, for in shifting the focus from philosophical inquiries into the nature of God and the world to the sociocultural and political function of the God concept, they offer some of the most compelling arguments for turning our backs on God, religion, and theological "thinking." For the writers in this study, it is atheism and not God that is a cause for hope, hope for political empowerment and democratic freedom for all people.

1

Frantz Fanon and J. Saunders Redding

The Psychological and Political Necessity of Atheism

"The church does not usually profess to be a group of ordinary human beings. It claims Divine Sanction. It professes to talk with God and to receive directly His Commandments. Its ministers and members do not apparently have to acquire Truth by bitter experience and long intensive study: Truth is miraculously revealed to them."

W.E.B. Du Bois, "The Color Line and the Church"

The title character of Jean Toomer's experimental short story "Kabnis" makes a rather odd remark about the Creator: "God, he doesn't exist, but nevertheless He is ugly. Hence, what comes from Him is ugly" (85). There are at least two things in this claim that should give an attentive reader pause. First, if God does not exist, then how can He be ugly? Only that which exists can be dubbed beautiful or ugly, and since God is, according to Kabnis, a nonexistent being, saying anything about the quality of His existence could only be an incoherent or nonsensical proposition. Putting aside for a moment the seeming contradiction of Kabnis's assertion, let us turn to the second, even more baffling part of his claim. How can Kabnis specifically justify calling God ugly? If anything, God has traditionally been configured as a spiritual comforter, the Good Shepherd, the loving Father, or the righteous One. Obviously, to call God ugly flies in the face of millennia of theological wisdom.

And yet, when examining the writings of prominent African American atheists, it is imperative that one have in place an intellectual framework that reconciles the seeming incoherence at the core of Kabnis's remark, for such writers consistently portray God, a being that does not exist for them, as a hideous entity. In this chapter, I offer a theoretical model that clarifies Kabnis's puzzling observation. This theory I derive from the writings of Frantz Fanon and J. Saunders Redding, two atheists who think that the primary function of the God concept is to justify racial oppression. But exposing this darker side of the God concept is no easy task, for as Ralph Ellison makes abundantly clear in the closing lines of his brilliant novel *Invisible Man*, social systems of injustice, which have been so effective in marginalizing and degrading culturally designated inferiors, sound at a frequency almost too low to be heard (581). Therefore, to make the oppressive structures of theism readily accessible to rational and enquiring minds, Fanon and Redding expose how the God concept, which for them is a sociopolitical construct and not an ontological reality, operates "on a level of subconsciousness" (Redding, *On Being Negro* 138).

"God! Bah!"

Nella Larsen, *Quicksand*

In *On Being Negro in America*, J. Saunders Redding rejects belief in God from a very distinct perspective: "I rejected God. Not my instincts, but my deepest feelings revolted compulsively—not because I was I, a sort of neutral human stuff reacting directly to experience, but because I was a Negro" (144). Were Redding an objective observer of the world (a Cartesian self-enthroned Subject or a Kantian Transcendental Ego of sorts), he would be able to claim that he accepts or rejects a concept like God from an unbiased vantage point. But as a man who has witnessed how "God and the word of God have been used to perpetuate the wicked idea of human inferiority" (147), he forgoes any pretense to objectivity or neutrality and instead acknowledges that he rejects God as a man of African descent. On the surface, such an admission should automatically disqualify Redding from making any intelligible comment about the God concept; after all, God is supposedly a being that transcends spatial, temporal, or cultural contingencies, so by acknowledging that he perceives the world through a culturally contingent ("Negro") lens instead of a transcultural metaphysical ("neutral human stuff") lens, Redding implicitly denies himself the possibility of knowing God. But for Redding, the God concept is nothing more than a human idea, "an implicit assumption in the thought of our age" (137). To know God, therefore, is to know what individuals within the culture have psychosemiotically projected into being or what the sociopolitical community has legitimized as Divine.[1] To paraphrase Zora Neale Hurston, God is a creature of our own minds (201), a conceptual being that assumes a provisional form in and through a semiotic sign.

Redding's specific motivation for rejecting God places him within a distinct tradition of atheist writers. One tradition is composed of epistemological skeptics.[2] After the Enlightenment shift from a theological to a rationalist/scientific mode of interpretive analysis, thinkers as varied as Baron d'Holbach, Ludwig Feuerbach, Charles Darwin, Leslie Stephen, Friedrich Nietzsche, Bertrand Russell, and Antony Flew have argued that, given the limits of the human capacity to know, it is impossible to say anything intelligible about the God concept.[3] In this tradition, it is the emergence and development of a rationalist, humanist-based epistemology that compelled so many respectable intellectuals to reject the God concept.

Redding certainly makes use of many of the interpretive methods of this particular tradition of atheist writers. For instance, he observes that implicit in "the fundamental concept of the Godhead is the idea of immutability" (147). But as Redding remarks, "Modern man's subtle modifications of the idea of God and the intellectual gymnastics that have made those modifications possible" (147) render belief in an immutable Deity highly questionable at best. Applying Nietzsche's genealogical method to theological systems exposes the God concept as a communal and cultural construction.[4] Therefore, Redding concludes, as did Feuerbach, that "the qualities attributed to God represent man's acknowledged needs" (146). Understanding that the God concept, instead of being an ontological reality that has been disclosed to humans or that humans have discovered, is actually a product of an individual or communal desire makes it nearly impossible for a rational person to take the traditional leap of faith.

However, while Nietzsche's genealogical method and Feuerbach's analysis of anthropomorphism have led many to reject the God concept, Redding is not such an atheist. Indeed, Redding belongs to a totally different tradition, one that takes politics as the basis and foundation for its rejection of belief. Let me bring these two divergent traditions into sharp focus. Epistemological skeptics claim that, given the limitations of the human psyche, rational humans cannot, in good conscience, believe in God.[5] Political atheists, however, argue that, given the way the God concept functions to justify political and sociocultural systems of oppression, responsible humans should not believe. This distinction, of course, begs the question: Why is belief in the God concept so politically objectionable? To answer this question, let us first turn to the writings of Frantz Fanon, the French-Martinican psychiatrist and political revolutionary, for he brilliantly exposes how the God concept has been strategically deployed to create a whole race of people as the wretched of the earth. While Fanon bases his theory primarily on his experiences in Martinique, France, Algeria, and Morocco, his insights are applicable to the situation of blacks in the United States.

"In the realm of power, Christianity has operated with an unmitigated arrogance and cruelty—necessarily, since a religion ordinarily imposes on those who have discovered the true faith the spiritual duty of liberating the infidels."

James Baldwin, *The Fire Next Time*

"Decolonization is the veritable creation of new men," Fanon claims in *The Wretched of the Earth*, but he qualifies this assertion by insisting that "this creation owes nothing of its legitimacy to any supernatural power" (36). The creation of the human in a decolonized context is much different than the creation of the human in a theological context. As Fanon observes only a few pages later, the "serf is in essence different from the knight, but a reference to divine right is necessary to legitimize this statutory difference" (40). The task at this point is to clarify the two distinctive forms of creation. Let me begin with the creation of the human within a theological framework.

Theists are epistemologically chosen. This means that they can see things that infidels cannot. In an epistemological sense, either the theist possesses a faculty of perception that the infidel does not or God discloses Himself and His Truths to the theist but not to the infidel. In the first letter to the Corinthians, Paul clearly articulates the distinction between the infidel and the theist, the natural man and the spiritual man. Theists have received a spirit from God that enables them to see spiritually, whereas infidels can only see material realities: "We speak of these, not in words of human wisdom but in words taught by the Spirit, thus interpreting spiritual things in spiritual terms. The natural man does not accept what is taught by the Spirit of God. For him, that is absurdity. He cannot come to know such teaching because it must be appraised in a spiritual way. The spiritual man, on the other hand, can appraise everything, though he himself can be appraised by no one" (1 Corinthians 2:13–15). Infidels will look but not see, listen but not hear. Until they take the leap of faith and accept the community's system of truth, unbelievers will not possess the epistemological faculty that enables theists to see what unbelievers cannot. Moreover, since theists can see from both a material and spiritual perspective, they can assess and judge the life of the infidel, whereas the theist's life is simply out of the infidel's epistemological reach. This means that, on a spiritual level of being, the world functions according to a logical and coherent system, but only theists have epistemological access to this system.

Significantly, from this spiritual perspective, things that would seem a contradiction to the average infidel are actually no contradiction at all to the theist. Let me give an example to illustrate this point. In the Old Testament, the Sixth Commandment reads, "Thou shalt not kill." But did God really mean this? When He delivered the Commandments atop Mount Sinai (Exodus 20), He was addressing the Israelites, and as we know, God commands the Chosen People to kill others with tenacious regularity. For instance, "If a man lies with a male as with a woman, both of them shall be put to death for their abominable deed" (Leviticus 20:13). Given the Old Testament context, homosexuality was considered an abomination, so we can understand why God should have responded so severely. But God does not sentence only the sexually "deviant" to death. He also sentences to death women who were not virgins before they were married (Deuteronomy 22:21–22). Of course, should a man "take" a woman before marriage, he is not sentenced to death; he is only forced to marry the woman he "took" (Deuteronomy 22:28–29). As for those who break the Sabbath, the Lord is pretty clear when he tells Moses: "This man shall be put to death; let the whole community stone him outside the camp" (Numbers 15:35). And should a son disobey his parents, then "all his fellow citizens shall stone him to death," as God instructs (Deuteronomy 21:18–21).

So God actually allows killing, according to this interpretation of the scriptures. He even commands His people to commit such acts, but, of course, only when individuals forfeit their right to life by violating God's law. But this is not quite true, for God does not sentence only criminals to death. For instance, God tells the Israelites to slaughter whole cities of people, sparing no one: "In the cities of those nations which the Lord, your God, is giving you as your heritage, you shall not leave a single soul alive. You must doom them all—the Hittites, Amorites, Canaanites, Perizzites, Hivites and Jebusites—as the Lord, your God, has commanded you" (Deuteronomy 20:16–18). Does dooming "them all" imply killing children and infants? This question is pertinent, for if God is just, He would not sentence to death those who are not yet capable of making responsible judgments. Therefore, couldn't we interpret "all" as meaning only those who have violated God's Laws? In other words, only the guilty ones? The God of Samuel, however, clarifies any confusion on this score: "This is what the Lord of hosts has to say: 'I will punish what Amalek did to Israel when he barred his way as he was coming up from Egypt. Go, now, attack Amalek, and deal with him and all that he has under the ban. Do not spare him, but kill men and women, children and infants, oxen and sheep, camels and asses'" (1 Samuel 15:2–3). Obviously, the scriptures do allow people to be killed who are not yet old enough to make informed decisions.

How is it possible for the Israelites to accept the Ten Commandments but not recognize that God commands them to violate one of those commandments quite regularly? There is a way to answer this question, but to do so, we must abandon our current understanding of the commandment "Thou shalt not Kill" as we raise a more fundamental question: who, according to traditional religious logic, was considered human? From Aristotle and Thomas Aquinas, who consider women "misbegotten males," to the Declaration of Independence in the United States, which does not include African Americans as part of "all men" who have the right to life and liberty, there has been a consistent logic with regard to personhood in western culture, a logic that can be traced back to the Chosen People mentality of the Judeo-Christian tradition. To be a people in the strict sense of the word, you must be chosen by God, but if you are not, you do not actually qualify for personhood. In the first letter of Peter, this Chosen People logic is articulated with absolute precision: "You, however, are 'a chosen race, a royal priesthood, a holy nation, a people he claims for his own to proclaim the glorious works' of the One who called you from darkness into his marvelous light. Once you were no people, but now you are God's people; once there was no mercy for you, but now you have found mercy" (1 Peter 2:9–11). Only chosen people can expect mercy. Obviously, the consequences for the nonchosen can be dire.[6] Not surprisingly, with regard to the treatment of nonchosen people, neither the Ten Commandments nor Christ's Golden Rule necessarily applies, since the nonchosen do not rise to the level of a people ("Once you were no people"). Therefore, were the Chosen People to steal from or kill the nonchosen, they would not necessarily be violating one of the Ten Commandments, for mercy is accorded only to people. This subtle qualification makes consistent sense of the seeming contradictions throughout the Bible.

The theist's spiritual perspective could only be considered quite maddening to those who suffer abuse at the hands of the chosen people. Because infidels can only see from a material vantage point, they cannot question or challenge the spiritual authority of the community of believers. Should they do so, the second letter of Peter explains how they should be treated: "They act like creatures of instinct, brute animals born to be caught and destroyed" (2 Peter 2:12). This claim does not necessarily imply that Christians should seek out and destroy nonbelievers. It is only when we read Deuteronomy, 1 Corinthians, and 1 and 2 Peter that the conditions for annihilating the infidel become clear. When the nonbeliever not only questions and challenges the believer's system of truth but also has a negative impact on the spiritual life of the chosen community, then the believers must annihilate the infidels, "lest they teach you to make any such abominable offerings as they make to their gods, and you thus sin against the Lord, your God" (Deuteronomy 20:18). Given this logic, if believers do not annihilate infidels, they are in danger of sinning against God. Moreover, because offending infidels are not people in the strict sense of the word (a "no people"), the believer would not be committing a crime by eliminating them—the Ten Commandments and Christ's Golden Rule apply only to humans.

In terms of creating humans, the believers are obviously in a privileged position—their epistemological chosenness leads to ontological chosenness. This system works on two levels. First, on the basis of a person's epistemological capacity, we can make some inferences about a person's ontological state of being. If a person can see spiritual things, then we can assume that this person is (ontologically) an earthly and spiritual being. But if a person cannot see spiritual things, then we can assume that this person is (ontologically) only an earthly being. And what constitutes spiritual realities? It cannot simply be a belief in God, for Deuteronomy 7 and 20 make it clear that all the Otherites believed in other gods. Therefore, it must be the specific truths and beliefs of the one and only true God, the God of those in power. Second, once the chosen people's epistemology is legitimized and internalized, they can begin the process of constructing the world and others in absolute terms. Stated more concretely, God communicates with believers but not infidels, and not surprisingly, believers are told that they are special beings, God's treasured possession, whereas the infidels are not.[7]

Infidels may want to question or challenge this claim, but since they lack a spiritual faculty of perception, they are not equipped to assess or judge the life of the believer. Logically, if the believer is both epistemologically and ontologically chosen, the infidel must be epistemologically and ontologically not chosen. This means that the infidel is a being that lacks a spiritual principle. As Paul says in 1 Corinthians 15:48, "The first man was of earth, formed from dust, the second is from heaven. Earthly men are like the man of earth, heavenly men are like the man of heaven." Given the earthly person's inability to see spiritual realities, it follows that this being belongs to a "no people" who can expect "no mercy," as it says in 1 Peter.

When Fanon refers to the appeal to divine right that legitimizes the essential differences between serf and knight, he is drawing our attention to the way the God concept has functioned in creating two types of humans, one superior and one inferior, one master and one slave.[8] For the believer, faith is the belief in something unseen, and since believers are specifically chosen, they have epistemological access to something inaccessible to infidels. In his discussion of the church, Fanon specifically draws his readers' attention to the chosen people discourse: "The Church in the colonies is the white people's Church, the foreigner's Church. She does not call the native to God's way but to the ways of the white man, of the master, of the oppressor. And as we know, in this matter many are called but few chosen" (*Wretched* 42). The church functions to instantiate the chosen people epistemology that subsequently enables the colonizers to define who is ontologically chosen and nonchosen. But the theological rhetoric here is twofold. First, the colonizers, who are spiritually chosen and can see what the nonchosen cannot, are superior because they can see. Second, what they see (what God communicates to them) is their spiritual superiority, their chosen status. Conversely, the natives are not chosen, as they lack the spiritual faculty of perception that would allow them to see spiritual things, but they are also not chosen because God has created them so, something they can neither verify nor reject because they cannot see what the colonizer/believer can see.[9]

This closed epistemological/ontological recursive loop is precisely what has such disastrous consequences for the colonized, according to Fanon. In the next paragraph, he details the logical consequences of the chosen people's theological system. The native is an animal, a nonspiritual being, a creature of the dust who cannot see heavenly things. In essence, the colonizer's theological discourse "turns" the native "into an animal" (42), just as 1 Peter claims that the nonchosen are a "no people" and just as 2 Peter claims that nonbelievers are like "brute animals." This animalizing discourse functions on three levels. First, on an epistemological level, the animal cannot perceive what the human can. So when the natives object to the oppressive system of colonization, the colonizers have at their disposal an extremely sophisticated system that justifies their actions. But to see the higher synthesis of the colonizers' system, a system that makes the colonizers' treatment of the colonized necessary, the native must rise to the colonizers' epistemological level: "As soon as the native begins to pull on his moorings, and to cause anxiety to the settler, he is handed over to well-meaning souls who in cultural congresses point out to him the specificity and wealth of western values" (43). There is a meaning and purpose behind the seeming injustices of the colonial system, and if the colonized would just put their trust in the well-meaning colonizers who have epistemological access to the logical principles of the system, the colonized would come to accept their western-prescribed condition of inferiority. In essence, the colonizers have access to a system of Truth that ultimately justifies colonization. But the colonized, who do not have epistemological access to this higher truth, must put their trust in the colonizers, for the colonizers are the only ones who understand the mystical tradition of western values. Not surprisingly, at a certain point, many of the colonized accept their inferior condition as a divine mandate: "A belief in fatality removes all blame from the oppressor; the cause of misfortunes and of poverty is attributed to God: He is fate. In this way the individual accepts the disintegration ordained by God, bows down before the settler and his lot, and by a kind of interior restabilization acquires a stony calm" (54–55). At this point, the theology of colonization has worked perfectly. The colonized are Paul's natural men of the earth who simply cannot see or understand the governing principles of western culture. In other words, because the colonized do not have access to the colonizer's God, they can neither verify nor reject the chosen/nonchosen discourse, so the colonized simply give up, admitting that their condition has been divinely prescribed. The God concept, shrouded in mystery, places the colonized at the mercy of the colonizer.

While turning the colonized into animals is important in order for the colonizers to deny the natives epistemological access to the secret truths of western values, it is also important for ontological reasons. Since the colonizers can know eternal verities, they can establish an objective standard that distinguishes good from evil, true from false. Not surprisingly, given the colonizer's privileged epistemological position, western values signify true morality and divine beauty, while the native's culture represents barbarism and depravity: "He [the native] is, let us dare to admit, the enemy of values, and in this sense he is the absolute evil." In essence, the native "is the depository of maleficent power, the unconscious and irretrievable instrument of blind forces" (41). Given their privileged position, the colonizers can ontologize the world and the other, and since the natives are merely earthly beings, they can neither question nor challenge the believers' truth system.

The last function of the animalizing discourse relates to violence. Thou shalt not kill! Love your neighbor as yourself! In principle, these claims sound compelling, but unfortunately, read within their historical and textual contexts, they contain a hidden premise that not only justifies but actually demands oppression and violence. In both the Old and New Testaments, God establishes an intimate relationship with his people, one based on direct communication. God is the one who specifically told his chosen people that you shall not kill and that you should love your neighbor as yourself. To preserve this intimate relationship with God, the chosen people must banish and/or destroy anything that could alienate the chosen people from their God. And should the chosen people come into contact with a nonchosen nonpeople, God not only sanctions but insists on genocide, "lest they teach you to make any such abominable offerings as they make to their gods, and you thus sin against the Lord, your God" (Deuteronomy 20:18). If contact with the natural man, the man of earth and dust, would spiritually infect the chosen people, and thereby make the chosen people less capable of communicating with their God, then the chosen people must destroy the natural man. Otherwise, the chosen people are in danger of becoming natural men themselves. As Fanon observes, the native "is the corrosive element, destroying all that comes near him; he is the deforming element, disfiguring all that has to do with beauty or morality" (41). Contact with the native can only have debilitating consequences for the chosen people: "All values, in fact, are irrevocably poisoned and diseased as soon as they are allowed in contact with the colonized race. The customs of the colonized people, their traditions, their myths—above all, their myths—are the very sign of that poverty of spirit and of their constitutional depravity" (42). By coming into contact with animalized humans, the spiritual people are in constant danger of having the nonchosen people's animalism rub off on them. For this reason, when the chosen people enter the unholy land, they must quarantine the animal element, subject the native to new values, and destroy anything that could infect the spiritual community. The colonizer is emotionally, psychologically, and spiritually obliged to conquer and destroy Evil.

Given this theological perspective, it would seem that all the animalized humans would have to do is to adopt western values and they would become a part of the chosen community. But therein lies the central cause of pathology in the chosen people mentality. Since the chosen people are in an intimate relationship with God, western laws and values will change in relation to the chosen community's ideological needs and desires. So as soon as the animalized native approaches becoming a chosen person, the chosen community can shift the truth-system such that it excludes the nearly chosen native. And since the native is still more animal than spirit, he or she cannot legitimately question or challenge the colonizer's newly constructed system of spiritual truth. Given this system, the native will always stand before the door of western law and truth, but will never gain access.[10] Within the theological framework of colonialism, the natives will always feel themselves to be animalized inferiors. Even if the chosen community were to ascribe personhood to the natives, they would still experience some form of pathological inferiority, because the colonizer's theological epistemology implies a stratification of humanness in which the colonizer is, by virtue of his or her epistemological capacity, more human than the colonized. Put simply, the colonizers are humans in the strict sense of the word because they, as beings created out of earth and spirit, can see what the native cannot—the very act of "seeing" what the infidel cannot implies the believer's/colonizer's ontological superiority. Therefore, becoming truly human for the native is in a perpetual state of deferral.

"White people hold the power, which means that they are superior to blacks (intrinsically, that is: God decreed it so), and the world has innumerable ways of making this difference known and felt and feared. Long before the Negro child perceives this difference, and even longer before he understands it, he has begun to react to it, he has begun to be controlled by it."

James Baldwin, *The Fire Next Time*

Understanding the way the God concept functions to determine humanness sheds considerable light on Fanon's and Redding's relentless critique of theology. For Redding, "God has been made to play a very conspicuous part in race relations in America" (137). But there are two separate and distinct ways that the God concept has "been used to perpetuate the wicked idea of human inferiority." On a conscious level, God makes explicit remarks about a person's or a group's ontological status in the world. For instance, black folk, as "the sons and daughters of Ham" (Larsen, *Passing* 159), have been created as "hewers of wood and drawers of water" (Larsen, *Quicksand* 3). These two claims are overt and direct, statements of seeming fact that can be ascribed to a certain person or group. At a conscious level, the discourse is readily accessible to all who understand the sentences.

However, these assertions, offensive as they are, do not concern Fanon and Redding very much. Rather, they are more concerned with the implicit function of the God concept and how it operates "on a level of subconsciousness" (Redding 138). This function relates to the believers' spiritual epistemology. To know a spiritual being like God, one must be a spiritual being. It might seem that all people are composed of matter and spirit, which would imply that all "people" would have the inborn potential to know a spiritual reality. But actually Paul indicates that some people are composed merely of earth (natural man), while others are composed of spirit and earth (spiritual man): "Earthly men are like the man of earth, heavenly men are like the man of heaven" (1 Corinthians 15:48). From this perspective, those who know a spiritual reality like God would be considered fully human, while those who do not would not be considered fully human. Given this epistemological model, a person's or a group's ontological condition is not determined by some spiritually authorized individual; no one has to state explicitly in the form of a clear proposition that "black folk are animals who lack a spiritual soul." Rather, the community of believers can infer that people of African descent are not spiritual beings on the basis of their inability to perceive a spiritual reality. And it is this inability, which remains unspoken and therefore subconscious, that justifies the white subjugation of people of African descent.

At this point, I want to use the frontispiece of Charles Carroll's book *Negro a Beast*, a popular theological work published in 1900 that embodies the pervasive theology in America, to shed more light on the way this theological model functions at the level of the subconscious. According to Carroll, what makes people human is their ability to have a "direct line of kinship with God." But this line of kinship does not extend to all beings. To give his reader a visual representation of the nature of kinship with the Divine, Carroll opens the book with an illustration of Adam and Eve in the Garden of Eden. Strategically placed at the center are the figures of Adam and Eve, whose whiteness extends into the Heaven as a symbol unifying the world's original parents with the Creator. Or, read from the other direction, the Creator, shrouded in heavenly whiteness, beams down His Divine essence to the original pair, thus uniting Himself in a bond of kinship with His creation. To the right looms a barely perceptible but ominous face, which, given the racist intent of the text, is supposed to be that of a black male or an ape. Carroll's essential point is embodied in the ambiguity. Both in terms of location and shading within the illustration, the person of African descent is prohibited from entering into a bond of kinship with God.

The argument of *Negro a Beast* is predicated on the idea of a spiritual faculty of perception. According to Carroll, there are three modes of creation: The earth is composed of matter, animals possess "physical and mental structures" (20), and humans consist of matter, mind, and the "spiritual, immortal life" (22), which is "a part of the substance of God" (23). Lacking a "spiritual" part, non- or subhumans "must be subject to accident, disease, decay, and final dissolution" (22). Since the African "simply stands at the head of the ape family, as the lion stands at the head of the cat family" (87), it follows that the black person is not in possession of the "spiritual, immortal life" and therefore contains within him- or herself no "part of the substance of God." In short, Carroll's black person is the Apostle Paul's natural man, a being that lacks a spiritual principle and thus cannot assess the life of the believer.

Illustration from *The Negro a Beast* by Charles Carroll. St. Louis: American Book and Bible House, 1900. Courtesy of Wellesley College Library Special Collections.

For Carroll, God has created within true humans a spiritual faculty, thereby establishing "between himself and man, the tie of kinship, which forms a bond of love and sympathy between them, and enables man to respect, confide in, and worship an all-wise, all-powerful, but invisible God" (181). Because whites possess this spiritual faculty, they can have a personal relationship with "a personal God" (12). By contrast, because blacks or "mixed-bloods" do not possess such a spiritual faculty, they cannot have a relationship with God.

In fact, since blacks do not possess a spiritual faculty, they do not qualify as humans, and as a consequence, they cannot have authentic knowledge.

At this point, Carroll is working within a well established western tradition. From Plato and Christ through Augustine and Aquinas to Kant and T. S. Eliot, knowledge is authentic and true only when it is not political or ideological. Edward Said insightfully exposes the idea on which this view is based. The assumption has been that 'true' knowledge is fundamentally nonpolitical (and conversely, that overtly political knowledge is not 'true' knowledge)" (*Orientalism* 10). Let me briefly indicate what is behind this view. Authentic knowledge is a pregiven, mind-independent reality, which, like its creator, is subject to neither the vicissitudes of the historical moment nor the vagaries of cultural context. For knowledge to be knowledge, it must be true for all people in all places at all times. But to access such knowledge, a person must possess a spiritual faculty of perception, an epistemological organ that, like its object, is bodiless and immutable. Therefore, the counter claim that "overtly political knowledge is not 'true' knowledge" is a logical extension of the true-knowledge philosophy. Were the faculty merely developed inside of humans within a cultural or historical context, it would be capable of apprehending only ideological or political knowledge, which is the culturally contingent knowledge of the institutions of power. Looked at from a slightly different angle, if there is no true, objective, metaphysical truth that is universally valid, then all knowledge would be a mere cultural construction, contingent and ephemeral at best, which would mean that it does not qualify as knowledge at all.

This true-knowledge philosophy, which figures prominently in the theological subjugation of culturally designated inferiors, is central to Carroll's book. The "law of God" (177) is "that the White must be the master of the Negro, else" the two races "can never live together in peace" (176–77). To know such a law, a person must "be endowed with mind almost God-like in its power; mind at once legislative, executive, and judicial" (96). It is this God-like mind, which is not subject to "final dissolution" and which can apprehend God's spiritual "Plan of Creation," that defines the human. Since blacks are animals, the kind of "mind" they have is subject to "final dissolution" and cannot apprehend any spiritual truth or concept. Therefore, they must always be inferior and subject to whites. Even blacks who have considerable white blood can never rise to the level of a spiritual being, because their animal-like subjectivity will make them forever incapable of apprehending the law of God. As Carroll claims, "If mated continuously with pure whites for millions of generations, you could never breed the ape out, nor breed the spiritual creation in, the offspring of Man and the Negro" (161). This view of the black person and mixed-bloods as apes explains why the African/ape figure in the frontispiece is both marginalized and ominous. Given the black person's lack of a God-like mind, he or she can never enter into that direct line of kinship between God and the white man. The black person will be forever marginalized.

But more important, should white people reach out to the black person, they would forever destroy the direct line of kinship between them and God, which would ultimately undermine the very Plan of Creation. Therefore, the black person poses a threat to the society's divine order, which white people are called upon to institute in and through a God-authorized political system.

It is such theological models as Carroll's that Redding has in mind when he claims that God and the word of God have been used to perpetuate the wicked idea of human inferiority. But it is important to note that Redding does not just claim that the God concept is used to justify dubbing black people inferior. He leaves open the possibility that it can be used to justify calling a wide range of people inferior, and a casual glance at the writings of prominent figures of the early twentieth century indicates that Redding's claim was not idiosyncratic. For instance, as a homosexual, E. M. Forster uses his novel *Maurice* to examine how the God concept was used to justify the animalization of all Oscar Wilde types. The novel, written in 1913–14, opens with Mr. Ducie, a senior schoolmaster, giving the title character an impromptu tutorial on the proper relationship between the sexes. To illustrate the only acceptable form of sexual union and communion, Ducie draws a diagram of a man and woman in the sand. After completing the lesson, "the poor old pedagogue" concludes with hardly containable enthusiasm: "It all hangs together—all—and God's in his heaven, All's right with the world. Male and female! Ah wonderful!" (15). By itself, this passage merely confirms what we already know, that many early twentieth-century schoolteachers had ridiculously simple and overly rigid notions of sexuality. But if we consider Ducie's remarks in relation to the philosophy of the clergyman of the novel, Mr. Borenius, then Ducie's comments would be much more pernicious than they might seem at first. For Borenius, human "conduct is dependent on faith," and consequently, "if a man is a 'bit of a swine' the cause is to be found in some misapprehension of God" (236). When he says "a bit of a swine," what Borenius really means is sexual perversion, for "when the nations went a whoring they invariably ended by denying God" (237). The structure of mind at work here is the same one in Carroll's frontispiece. There are certain people (whites/heterosexuals) who have the epistemological capacity to apprehend a moral law mandated by God. By contrast, there are some (blacks/sexual "deviants") who lack this capacity and thus, as immoralists, stand outside the direct line of kinship between God and man. Given the absence of this spiritual faculty, sexual deviants are not entirely human; they are "a bit of a swine," an animal reference that certainly recalls Carroll's picture of the marginalized African/ape.

To cast a person or a group of people outside the direct line of kinship between God and man, it is not necessary to reduce the person or the group to an animal. All that is necessary is to demonstrate that certain people lack a spiritual faculty of perception. Such is the strategy the black preacher, Reverend Pleasant Green, deploys in order to cast women outside the line of kinship in Nella Larsen's *Quicksand*. After her conversion, Helga Crane, the novel's cosmopolitan protagonist, assumes the role of a traditional southern housewife, which consists of having a garden, pigs, and chickens. All of this, along with a husband, results in her being right with God (120). But after birthing three children and living for two years as a domestic drudge, Helga begins to question the role assigned to her. According to Green, however, such questioning is unacceptable and unjustified, for as a minister of the Lord, he "was concerned only with things of the soul, spiritual things" (115). He knows God's will, which enables him to say with certainty that Helga's discontent is "an act of God" (125). Indeed, it is his spiritual faculty of perception that allows him to know God's will. As a woman, Helga apparently has no such capacity, which implicitly casts her on the margins of the bond of kinship between God and man. Therefore, if she wants to do God's will, she must submit, in all humility, to the dictates of her husband.

While Forster and Larsen create characters who use the God concept to justify violence, oppression, and abuse, to critique the theological structure of mind, T. S. Eliot actually uses the God concept in order to justify banishing a particular group from the culture. Following the apostle Paul, Eliot asserts "the primacy of the supernatural over the natural life" ("Religion" 108). This supernatural/natural distinction necessitates two types of knowledge, which Eliot defines in terms of tradition and orthodoxy. For Eliot, tradition is "a way of feeling and acting which characterizes a group throughout generations" (*After* 31), so it "is of the blood, . . . rather than of the brain" (32). By contrast, "*orthodoxy* is a matter which calls for the exercise of all our conscious intelligence." In other words, where a tradition can exist only in the context of a human community, orthodoxy can exist even if there are no

humans. Eliot is unambiguous on this point: "While tradition, being a matter of good habits, is necessarily real only in a social group, orthodoxy exists
whether realized in anyone's thought or not" (32). And as a Christian, Eliot
specifically calls for a tradition of "Christian orthodoxy" (22). To apprehend
Eliot's Christian orthodox Truth, one must be capable of "spiritual perception," and if a person poses a threat to the orthodox community, then Eliot
suggests banishment. As he claims in *After Strange Gods*: "Reasons of race and
religion combine to make any large number of free-thinking Jews undesirable"
(22). For Eliot, contact with those nonorthodox races and religions would
threaten the purity of spiritual perception and thereby make orthodox truth,
which God created, inaccessible. So it is imperative that the orthodox community cast out unorthodox individuals. Failure to do so would threaten the
bond of kinship between God and man.[11]

I only supply three examples here, but I could have easily included Joseph
Conrad's *Heart of Darkness* or *Lord Jim*, Forster's *Howards End* or *A Passage
to India*, or Virginia Woolf's *Mrs. Dalloway*, *Orlando* or *The Waves*, for each
of these works examines the same dynamic: the claim that there exists a spiritual, nonideological Truth, which only those beings with a spiritual faculty of
perception can apprehend. Given their ability to know such nonideological
truths, the spiritual beings are in a position to cast nonspiritual beings in slave-
like roles within the culture, and if the nonspiritual beings resist, violence,
marginalization, or banishment is not just allowed but is psychologically and
politically necessary. Of course, the nonspiritual beings (blacks, mixed-bloods,
homosexuals, women, Jews, Patusanis, Indians, Africans, Moors, wealthy people, poor people, etc.) will differ on the basis of those in positions of power,
but the dynamic is always the same. It is this dynamic which functions at the
level of the subconscious.

So let me make a clear distinction at this point between the conscious and
subconscious functions of the God concept. That there is a Divine Being who
has created humans with the capacity to know Him and His laws is the primary subconscious function of the God concept. Such an assumption leads
to the belief that there is such a thing as proper or authentic knowledge that
can be discovered by those select humans who have the requisite faculty of
perception or the appropriate orientation toward knowledge. The secondary
assumption is based on a stratification of humanness, which is determined by
a person's ability to apprehend authentic knowledge. Once these assumptions
are ingrained at the level of the subconscious, it then becomes possible to formulate, at the conscious level, who has the requisite epistemological capacity

for obtaining authentic knowledge, the kind of knowledge that is necessary for ruling and governing the body politic. To put this in Baldwin's words: "White people hold the power, which means that they are superior to blacks (intrinsically, that is: God decreed it so), and the world has innumerable ways of making this difference known and felt and feared." For instance, in Carroll's America, because white males can know God and/or His laws, they are the best equipped to rule and govern. By contrast, since black people cannot have authentic knowledge, they must be ruled and governed. This conscious formulation will differ from region to region, so in Forster's England, it is heterosexuals who are equipped to rule and govern, while homosexuals must be ruled and governed. In T. S. Eliot's Europe, Christians are the chosen people, while Jews are the epistemologically challenged. At the level of the subconscious, the theological model is the same from one place to the next, but at the conscious level, the formulation will vary from one place to the next.

For Fanon and Redding, it is when the God concept functions at the level of the subconscious that it is most destructive for culturally designated inferiors. As politically disempowered figures, people of African descent feel that they cannot contribute to the construction of the body politic. Here's how the system works. White people, who have access to God's Truth, can define people and the world, while black people, who have a limited epistemological capacity, can only be defined.[12] In short, the God concept enables those in power to be politically active, creators and definers of the body politic. Conversely, the God concept and the attendant spiritual epistemology divest culturally designated inferiors of intellectual and political agency, reducing them to mere objects (things) to be controlled and defined.

Consequently, the God concept has made African Americans feel paralyzed. As Redding claims, "But God has changed, and though man himself has wrought these changes, he has declared them God's own changes and therefore factors, equations, and of a piece with the mysterious and unknowable nature of God. Indeed, God's very supernaturalness, His mysteriousness and inscrutability ('God moves in mysterious ways His wonders to perform,' *ergo* 'we cannot know God's purpose in making the black race inferior to the white,' and we cannot 'fathom the repulsion which God has given one race for another, or one people for another') are largely modern attributions" (147). Being dubbed inferior is only a secondary problem in this passage; primary is exclusion from the closed epistemological/ontological recursive loop, which leads to paralysis and ultimately psychosis. Notice how the logic in this passage unfolds. God has changed, but it is those in power who have "wrought these changes." This is a very cynical observation. The traditional view, that authentic knowledge is immutable and universal, is exposed as a sham. God takes his cue from humans, specifically those who control the culture's intellectual resources. For the culturally marginalized and dispossessed, God is, not surprisingly, a mysterious and unknowable being, but also a being that makes absolute proclamations. This view of God, no doubt, effectively dispossesses these individuals from contributing to the culture's political vision. But as I have been trying to argue throughout this chapter, the primary problem is not the surface racism ("We cannot know God's purpose in making the black race inferior to the white"). The problem is the subconscious belief that there is a God-created Truth to which certain people have privileged access. Since the culturally marginalized *feel* that they lack the requisite epistemological capacity to know God and his Laws (they are mysterious and inscrutable), in other words, since the dispossessed accept, at the level of the subconscious, the view of authentic knowledge which they cannot access, they do not make an effort to construct God or knowledge, and as a consequence, they are vulnerable to being constructed as inferiors.

Let me articulate the consequences of the recursive loop within a political context. Let us say, just for the sake of argument, that those in power say: God decrees that all people, irrespective of race, are human in the strict sense of the word and therefore possess the inalienable human rights of life, liberty, and the pursuit of happiness. For Fanon and Redding, such a declaration, instead of indicating that the culture has overcome a dehumanizing system, would actually reinforce and confirm the dehumanizing system. Those in power actively construct and define the political (they know Truth and therefore behave like true humans by defining the world), and while they may accord culturally designated inferiors human or equal rights, they have still not allowed the marginalized figures to participate in the construction and definition of the political. At the core of the recursive loop is an irreconcilable dilemma: the white believer defining (the definition would be articulated on a conscious level) the black infidel as fully human confirms (on a subconscious level, since the white believer assumes that he or she is authorized to be the definer) for the white person that the black person is not fully human. For the atheists in this study, it is not enough to be defined as humans; the culture needs to adopt a conceptual system that empowers all people to behave "human," as active creators and definers of the political, and since the epistemological/ontological recursive loop of theology implicitly legitimizes one group's truth over another's, and thereby defines some people as more human than others, the system itself necessarily disempowers another group—it does not allow culturally designated inferiors to rise above the level of the defined thing. And since the culturally designated inferior is a being that lacks the epistemological capacity to question or challenge the God-created concept that those in power know, the disempowered person must simply submit to the unfathomable and inscrutable decrees of God, decrees that "man himself has wrought."

As should be clear, positing God's existence leads to a major problem with regard to intellectual agency. God has told the white theist that the black race is inferior to the white. This assertion functions on both the conscious and subconscious levels. On the conscious level, the proposition is clear: whites are superior to blacks because God says so. This is an overt claim that all people can understand. On the subconscious level, whites, who possess a spiritual faculty of perception, can communicate with God, so they can determine (hence their intellectual agency) what God's will is. As beings in communication with God, white folk are definers, not the defined. Conversely, blacks, who do not possess a spiritual faculty of perception, cannot communicate with God, so they cannot determine (hence their lack of intellectual agency) what God's will is. In essence, it is by controlling the God concept that one can experience intellectual agency.

Had Redding and Fanon been less responsible and astute intellectuals, they would have focused their attention on the surface elements of the theological model. In other words, they would have countered the absurdly racist arguments of people like Carroll and argued that black people possess a spiritual faculty of perception and are therefore full-fledged human beings who have the epistemological (spiritual) capacity to access authentic knowledge. But they both realized that such an approach would do nothing to demolish the subconscious apparatus that makes the wicked idea of human inferiority possible. Therefore, instead of clumping new groups of people into the Divine/human bond of kinship, and thereby justifying the full-fledged humanness of a larger segment of the population, Fanon and Redding reject the theological model. The problem with the God concept for the atheists in this study is that it authorizes the existence of a mind-independent concept which only full-fledged humans can access. So for these atheists, even if they could convincingly argue that they have the epistemological capacity to access authentic knowledge, thus justifying their status as full-fledged humans, this would do nothing to dismantle the apparatus that can and will be used to dub other people and groups sub- or nonhuman. In other words, because atheists like Fanon and Redding are concerned with human rights more generally, they seek to expose the apparatus that has been used to subjugate, marginalize, and dehumanize a variety of people within the culture. As Fanon argues in *Black Skin, White Masks*, the same structures that are used to degrade and violate black people have been used against the Jews (121–23). Or, as Redding claims, the God concept is used not just to dub black people inferior but to perpetuate the wicked idea of human inferiority. To make the stratification of all or any humans impossible, Fanon and Redding renounce the God concept and its logical offspring, authentic knowledge. In its stead, they reconfigure knowledge as psychosemiotic construction, a product of language and the mind. Indeed, only by adopting a philosophy of knowledge as human constructed, which would mean that God would also be a culturally constructed concept, could the society overcome the dehumanizing structures implicit in the theological model of authentic knowledge.

In essence, we could, ironically, place Fanon and Redding (and, for that matter, all the writers in this study) in the black liberation theology tradition, which includes writers like David Walker and James Cone. The "central commitment" of liberation theology, John Ernest claims, is "action *in* the world," and consequently it "is a theology of praxis, of an ongoing process of action and reflection" (16) "in the service of ongoing and concrete systemic reform" (18). Given its appreciation and understanding of Marx's political analysis of culture, liberation theology seeks to expose and subsequently eradicate the ideological structures of oppression. But as Cone claims, while liberation theologians focus on "the liberation struggle" of people within their own communities, they are also deeply concerned about the "oppressed peoples fighting for freedom through the world" (*Speaking* 40–41). Ultimately, liberation theology's goal is a comprehensive experience of individual and communal agency, the capacity for self-definition, self-determination, and self-creation. I find Ernest's articulation of its objective most insightful, though he revises it slightly to suit his historiographic project: "Liberation historiography . . . is an attempt to liberate African Americans from an other-defined history so as to provide them with agency in a self-determined understanding of history—and since the ultimate determination of historical authority and agency was God's," comprehensive agency must be conceived within "a larger and largely unknowable narrative of providential history" (18). The writers in *African American Atheists and Political Liberation* would find in liberation theologians like-minded comrades who share a similar dream of political and communal autonomy, with one very notable exception: they would argue that the God concept is the problem and thus cannot be part of the solution. Therefore, we could say that the writers in this study evolve a liberation antitheology or a liberation atheism, a project committed to creating the ideological conditions for African Americans to have a comprehensive experience of personal and communal agency, but which could only be realized through an atheistic vision of social justice.

"It should seem that Negroes, of all Americans, would be found in the Freethought fold since they suffered more than any other class of Americans from the dubious blessings of Christianity."
Hubert H. Harrison, "On a Certain Conservatism in Negroes"

Seeing the way the God concept intellectually and politically disables culturally designated inferiors explains why both Redding and Fanon seek to abolish theology and the God concept. For both writers, killing God is an intellectual and psychological must in order to set into motion an entirely new system of creating humans.[13] According to the believers' model, there is such a thing as human nature, the believers have access to this nature, and given their privileged epistemological position, they are conveniently dubbed ontologically superior. If there is no God, however, the believers' appeal to the divine would be nothing more than a manipulative ploy for creating themselves as superior, a rhetorical will to power that can only have disastrous consequences for those who do not control the culture's intellectual means of subject-production. To make it impossible, therefore, for colonizers and believers to conceal their will to power over others, Fanon and Redding favor an atheistic philosophy of self-creating, one that makes an appeal to God or truth both impossible and irrelevant.

According to this view, knowledge is psychological projection rather than accurate representation; it is an epistemic construction of the will instead of an objective discovery of the intellect. For this reason, in the best of all worlds, which would be a decolonized one, Fanon's post-God human would be in a perpetual state of flux, forever becoming instead of ever being. In a post-God world, the human exists as a rhythm rather than a static thing: "It [decolonization] brings a natural rhythm into existence, introduced by new men, and with it a new language and a new humanity. Decolonization is the veritable creation of new men. But this operation owes nothing of its legitimacy to any supernatural power; the 'thing' that has been colonized becomes man during the same process by which it frees itself" (36–37). The thing is named into being, whereas the human comes into being the moment it takes its humanity, the moment it casts off the theological model ("this operation owes nothing of its legitimacy to any supernatural power") and begins the process of creating and defining itself. But naming self into being cannot be seen in terms of a final self because the new language and new humanity exist as a rhythm rather than a being. As a subject, the decolonized and detheologized human projects self into being, but existing as a rhythm, it must be open to deconstruction and reconstruction, a never-ending process. For Fanon, to be human means being that which creates and defines but which can never be finally created or ultimately defined. To define the human is to reduce it to a thing, to *subject* it to an imprisoning discourse. Such an experience reduces the human to an object without agency, something that is acted upon rather than acting. Put simply, theology and colonization imply a pernicious fatalism for those who do not control the intellectual means of subject production. For the natives who suffer under the yoke of theology and colonization, they have only two options: either nihilistic despair, which leads to pathology and/or neurosis, or violent revolution, a thorough rejection of the colonizers and their theological system.

According to this decolonized and detheologized system of self-creation and definition, truth suffers the same fate as God: "The problem of truth ought also to be considered. In every age, among the people, truth is the property of the national cause. No absolute verity, no discourse on the purity of the soul, can shake this position" (50). People should not be subject to God-created Truth or God as Truth; rather, truth should be at the service of the people, specifically the people's national cause. In the world of theology and colonization, truth as a God-given, preexistent reality is the most effective instrument for justifying a ruthless system of oppression. For Fanon, therefore, the most hideous forms of oppression and human rights violations can only occur in a theological world in which Truth exists. Since believers (colonizers) have access to truth, we can infer that they are ontologically superior, constructed such that they can perceive the highest realities, like true morality and real justice. Since unbelievers (colonized) do not have access to truth, we can infer that they are ontologically inferior, constructed such that they cannot see the highest realities. But if we tear away the veils of God and truth, colonization would be exposed: "Colonialism is not a thinking machine, nor a body endowed with reasoning faculties. It is violence in its natural state" (61). The primary violence of colonialism is theological, the semiotic violence of constructing the colonizer (believer) as a spiritual being, who has epistemological access to God, and the colonized (unbeliever) as a material being, who cannot appraise the world in a spiritual way. Once this system is set into motion, the rest is a foregone conclusion.

According to this view of theology, God and Truth are only politically empowering for those who control the intellectual means of subject-production, in other words, for colonizers and believers, those who have epistemological access to what the colonized infidels cannot see. For the natives who attend to the function of "the inevitable religion" (67) of colonialism, God and Truth can only be a source of horror, the instruments that justify the natives' subservient condition: "For the native, objectivity is always directed against him" (77). Understanding how the theological mentality has effectively justified abuse of the culturally designated inferior explains why Hubert H. Harrison believes "that Negroes, of all Americans, would be found in the Freethought fold since they suffered more than any other class of Americans from the dubious blessings of Christianity." Fanon shares Harrison's view, which is why he claims that the "motto 'look out for yourself,' the atheist's method of salvation, is in this [colonial] context forbidden" (47). Atheism unmasks God and Truth: there is no spiritual epistemology, there are no mystical values, and, above all, there is no God. Such thinking is, understandably, forbidden in the world of theology and colonization. But for Fanon and Redding, it is only in the atheist's world that we will be able to escape subjugation, a world in which humans will be free to produce a living rhythm predicated on creating and defining themselves. In other words, until we expose the lie of theology, we will never eliminate the "wicked idea of human inferiority."

"As a Negro who has grown up in the United States, I believe that belief in God has hurt my people."

James Forman, "God Is Dead: A Question of Power"

God does not exist, yet belief in Him has caused unspeakable suffering and psychological damage, which explains why He is ugly nevertheless. Such is the logic of Kabnis's remark in Toomer's short story and Forman's comment in the above epigraph. For Fanon and Redding, positing the existence of a spiritual reality that only a certain group of people can see necessarily leads to a stratification of humanness that ultimately perpetuates the wicked idea of human inferiority. Moreover, because the putative spiritual reality is accessible only to a certain group of people, it leads to the construction of a closed epistemological/ontological recursive loop, a conceptual system that allows only certain people within the culture to behave as independent intellectual agents. Conversely, such a system renders culturally designated inferiors incapable of behaving as independent agents—it implicitly converts them into subhumans, three-fifth humans, or animals. It should come as no surprise, therefore, that Fanon and Redding reject theology and the God concept. Admitting that all knowledge is human constructed, instead of created by God, is the most important step toward *making* all people "human." For Fanon and Redding, atheism is a psychological and political must for the construction of a pluralist democracy and the possibility of social justice.

2

The Humanist/Atheist Controversy
in Richard Wright's *The Outsider*

"God, of course, is an implicit assumption in the thought of our age."
J. Saunders Redding, *On Being Negro in America*

Redding's and Fanon's critiques of a theological approach to constructing and defining the human and nonhuman occurred at a time when the concept of the human and the philosophy of humanism were simultaneously undergoing radical developments and being totally undermined. From the twentieth-century humanist perspective, the intellectual movement finally found a coherent synthesis in its two manifestos (published in 1933 and 1973) and in the lucid and accessible work of Corliss Lamont, a Columbia philosophy professor who published *Humanism as a Philosophy* in 1949. An optimistic, world-affirming system that advocates "the methods of reason, science, and democracy," humanism, according to Lamont, makes use of a variety of intellectual resources to understand "the various aspects of human nature" so that it can ultimately promote "this-worldly happiness, freedom, and progress for all" (12–13). Ironically, just two years before the publication of Lamont's book, Jean-Paul Sartre penned his famous essay "The Humanism of Existentialism." While Lamont bases his humanism on a rigorous understanding of human nature, Sartre rejects the concept of human nature as a fiction that became obsolete after God's death: "Thus, there is no human nature, since there is no God to conceive it" (36). Responding in large measure to Sartre's humanism, Martin Heidegger published his groundbreaking "Letter on Humanism," an essay that blatantly opposes humanism because "the highest determinations of the essence of man in humanism still do not realize the proper dignity of man" (210).

Significantly, these debates about humanism were in full force, specifically in relation to existentialism, precisely when Richard Wright was composing his novel *The Outsider*, which he started in 1946 or 1947. Steeped in the writings of Edmund Husserl (Heidegger's *Doktorvater*) and Heidegger, in close contact with Sartre and his companion, Simone de Beauvoir, and much impressed with Albert Camus's novel *The Stranger* (which could also be translated from the French as *The Outsider*), Wright made his contribution to the ongoing debate about humanism through his fiction, though he did so from his distinctive subject position as an African American atheist. Before I turn to *The Outsider*, however, I need to provide an intellectual backdrop for understanding Wright's work, one that takes into account the broad range of influences on his thinking. And yet a simple survey of key intellectual precursors is certainly not enough to understand Wright's 1953 novel, for he had an amazing capacity to identify vulnerable assumptions within conceptual systems, so engagement with and usage of specific philosophical systems is never a matter of mere appropriation. Therefore, my depiction of the intellectual backdrop, humanism in this case, will be done in anticipation of Wright's critique and endorsement of humanism.

"At the end of formal humanism and philosophic renunciation, there is Hitler."

Aimé Césaire, *Discourse on Colonialism*

Naturalistic, never supernaturalistic; human-centered, never God-centered; this-worldly, never other-worldly—these are some of the foundational precepts of humanism, according to Lamont. Put simply, "Humanism, having its ultimate faith in man, believes that human beings possess the power or potentiality of solving their own problems, through reliance primarily upon reason and scientific method applied with courage and vision" (13). Given humanism's radical affirmation of the human, it supports "democracy, peace, and a high standard of living on the foundations of a flourishing economic order, both national and international" (14). Moreover, it believes "in democratic procedures, parliamentary government, with full freedom of expression and civil liberties, throughout all areas of economic, political, and cultural life" (14).

While it is certain that humanists, like Lamont, see the death of God as an essential and positive development that leads, quite logically, to the emergence of humanism, there is another school of thought that contends that the atheistic turn in the western intellectual tradition leads to the death of the human.[1] To quote one of the most prominent French poststructuralists, "[I]t is not so much the absence or the death of God that is affirmed as the end of man" (Foucault, *Order* 385). Let me briefly trace some of the intellectual developments that led to the erasure of the human.

It is a given that the human, per definition, is clearly distinct from an animal and a machine. Endowed with reason, capable of self-determination, and conscious of consciousness, the human, in contrast to animals, has the ability to overcome the mechanistic laws of natural necessity and the capacity to act as a rational, moral, and therefore free agent.[2] Such was the tale of the eighteenth-century human, that being who sits squarely between the heavenly host and the unthinking brutes.[3] By the nineteenth century, however, there was, as Paul Sheehan rightly observes, "a turn away from the human as a *given* towards the human as a *problem*" (181). For Sheehan, with the emergence of Arthur Schopenhauer's philosophy of a primordial will as the determinate force of being and Charles Darwin's dethroning of nature's most godlike creature through evolution, the human has been reduced to either an inhuman machine or an inhuman animal. In either case, something inhuman not only controls but also props up human identity.

Edward Said tells a similar tale, though he features different characters. Rene Descartes grounded his human and humanism in the *cogito*, the autonomous thinking faculty that enables humans to have ahistorical, mind-independent knowledge. But writers like Karl Marx and Sigmund Freud effectively exposed the Cartesian cogito as a charming humanistic fiction by identifying systems that undermined the cogito's autonomy. Said notes that "the existence of systems of thinking and perceiving transcended the powers of individual subjects, individual humans who were inside those systems (systems such as Freud's 'unconscious' or Marx's 'capital') and therefore had no power over them, only the choice either to use or be used by them. This, of course, flatly contradicts the core of humanistic thought, and hence the individual *cogito* was displaced, or demoted, to the status of illusory autonomy or fiction" (*Humanism* 9–10). Nature, evolution, capitalism, the unconscious—these are just a few forces and systems that radically undermined the human's sovereign position in the universe.

What distinguishes antihumanist traditions is the way they function to undermine the established definition of the human. For Enlightenment rationalists, the human will is subject to human reason, and given the human's privileged position in the scale of being, the human is the monarch of inhuman creation. But for Schopenhauer, Darwin, Marx, and Freud, the presence of the inhuman within the human compromised the semantic integrity of the traditionally defined human. In other words, given discoveries and advances in philosophy, science, politics, and psychology, the traditional definition of the human falls apart, the semantic center of humanism cannot hold, and anarchy is loosed upon the human-ordered scale of being.

For poststructuralists, these antihumanist traditions did less to undermine the human than they did to expose the concept of the human as a sociopolitical construct. This constructivist tradition is less concerned with correctly signifying that "bare-forked animal" that rules the planet than it is with the construction of the signifying systems used to represent the seemingly rational animal. The traditional view of language, which stands in stark contrast to the constructivist tradition, holds that the true word incarnates the thing that it names.[4] According to this view, there is a proper word to signify an object in the world, an objective word that neutrally represents mind-independent objects. This true word is no mere invention; it is not tainted by an individual or communal will to exert rhetorical power over that which is represented. Rather, the true word, which leads to true knowledge, is a precise, accurate, and objective representation of that which it names. For practitioners of this view of language, true knowledge is either a logical semiotic extension of the thing represented or an accurate representation that has been extracted from a Heaven of Ideas. In either case, true knowledge cannot be debased by being dubbed a mere human construction.

For constructionists, by contrast, no matter how compelling, no matter how useful, discourse is always societally and culturally constructed. Such is the basis of Sartre's rejection of the idea of human nature and morality: "The existentialist . . . thinks it very distressing that God does not exist, because all possibility of finding values in a heaven of ideas disappears along with Him; there can no longer be an *a priori* Good, since there is no infinite and perfect consciousness to think it" (40–41). Because there is no transcendent being that authorizes, legitimizes, or guarantees the existence of an objective and neutral concept, humans must acknowledge that they, from their culturally and societally biased perspectives, construct all words and sentences and are therefore the originators of all truth systems. Given this view, concepts like the human and humanism must be considered societal and cultural constructs, and not ontological realities that are waiting to be discovered.

Recognizing that all concepts, the productions of reason, are arbitrary constructions that falsify being, Heidegger thinks it better to dispense with words like *humanism* (195). The reason is this: Being is more primordial than a concept like the human. If the primary objective is to understand the truth of Being, then philosophy needs to resist the impulse to be satisfied with such simple, formulaic, and overrated concepts like the human. This does not mean that Heidegger sees individual humans as insignificant beings. To the contrary, once humans discover that they are "not the lord[s] of beings" but "the shepherd[s] of Being" (221), they will gain much more than their humanity; they will attain "the truth of Being" (221). By reifying the human and humanism, by converting such words into metaphysical concepts (202), humans and humanism have contented themselves with phantoms of the imagination, projected specters of language and the mind. So Heidegger rejects humanism in order to achieve a much nobler destiny than humanism could ever fathom.

Like Sartre and Heidegger, Derrida and Jean-Francois Lyotard reject the idea of a neutral and objective conceptual reality (like humanism or the human) that humans can know and define through reason, but their critique of such a concept is based on a political view of knowledge, and as a consequence, the tone in their writing is much harsher and more cynical. As Lyotard puts it, humanism is, among other things, "a marketing operation" (2). For those committed to humanism, such a comment can only seem absurd if not downright offensive. But Lyotard is not being glib. As I have already argued in the first chapter, whoever is in control of the intellectual means of production can determine humanness, and just as theists have used a spiritual epistemology to explicitly and implicitly dub some people human and others not human, so too have humanists used a rationalist epistemology to do the same.[5] For Lyotard, it is the culture industry that ultimately constructs humans as human by forcing individuals to interiorize "the interests and values of civilization" (4). Children, therefore, who *lack* "full humanity," are in desperate need of the culture industry, for the "institutions which constitute culture supplement this native lack" of the child (3). Using Lyotard's approach to the human, we should not be asking, What is the human? Rather, we should be asking: How has the culture industry decided to construct the concept of the human in order to achieve its specific objectives? What the human is in and of itself becomes a ridiculous question in the constructionist's world. No doubt, such an approach to the human significantly undermines the authority, legitimacy, and value of a movement, like humanism, that is based on a proper understanding of the human.

While Richard Wright certainly knew about the raging debate concerning humanism and the human, he approached the debate from a unique and complicated perspective. As an African American atheist, Wright understood how humanism could secure civil liberties and equal rights for culturally marginalized individuals, so Anthony B. Pinn, who claims that "humanism . . . has served as a grounding for liberative action within African American history," is right to include the author of *The Outsider* in his volume *By These Hands: A Documentary History of African American Humanism* (10). But as a

man of African descent, Wright also witnessed the way humanism has functioned to justify marginalizing and abusing certain individuals within the culture. To clarify this second, uncharitable interpretation of humanism, let me
briefly turn to Aimé Césaire, the French Martinican poet who helped launch
the journal *Presence Africaine*.[6]

In 1950, Césaire published *Discourse on Colonialism*, an essay that tries to
expose the political psychology that has enabled Europeans to justify to others
and themselves the brutal exploitation and colonization of nonwhite, non-European cultures. After a casual reading of this work, a reader might think that
the essay was incorrectly titled, for Césaire spends much of his time analyzing
Hitler's atrocities in Europe. But for Césaire, what Hitler did in Europe from
1933 to 1945 was no mere aberration; it was the logical product of Europe's
philosophical worldview, which has justified colonization. And what was that
philosophical Weltanschauung? Primarily humanism and Christianity. Let me
quote a long sentence that clearly articulates Césaire's shocking view:

> [I]t would be worthwhile to study clinically, in detail, the steps taken by
> Hitler and Hitlerism and to reveal to the very distinguished, very hu-
> manistic, very Christian bourgeois of the twentieth century that without
> his being aware of it, he has a Hitler inside him, that Hitler *inhabits* him,
> that Hitler is his *demon*, that if he rails against him, he is being inconsis-
> tent and that, at bottom, what he cannot forgive Hitler for is not *crime*
> in itself, *the crime against man*, it is not *the humiliation of man as such*,
> it is the crime against the white man, the humiliation of the white man,
> and the fact that he applied to Europe colonialist procedures which until
> then had been reserved exclusively for the Arabs of Algeria, the "coolies"
> of India, and the "niggers" of Africa. (8)

Like Lyotard, Césaire understands how European humanism presupposes a
"native lack" within uncivilized others. Until the uncivilized others interiorize
certain European-legitimated moral precepts and intellectual faculties, they
will not qualify as humans in the strict sense of the word. The tacit assumptions implicit in humanism convert the nonwhite, non-European into an animal or a thing: "colonization = 'thingification'" (21). Therefore, humanism,
by establishing a definition of what is properly human, implicitly identifies
certain individuals as nonhuman, and thereby necessitates and justifies the
ennobling practices of colonizing and ultimately humanizing the savage races.
Without the European humanist's civilizing efforts, inferior "peoples" would
not realize their destiny of becoming fully human. And should uncivilized

nonhumans resist the colonizers' gift of true civilization and humanness, exterminating the brutes becomes a moral and political must.

According to Césaire, Hitler applied to Jews and other Europeans the dehumanizing philosophy of humanism that Europeans have used against non-Europeans, which is why Césaire concludes: "At the end of formal humanism and philosophic renunciation, there is Hitler" (15). Since the definition of the human is variable, it can be used to include a broad range or a narrow group of people. It all depends on who controls the intellectual means of production. What Hitler did was to circumscribe the human so narrowly that it excluded certain whites and Europeans whose humanity was generally taken for granted. By manipulating the concept of the true human, Hitler reduced fellow Europeans to animals and things, and this, argues Césaire, was the logical product of Europe's humanist philosophy.

How, then, are we to reconcile Pinn's claim that "humanism . . . has served as a grounding for liberative action within African American history" and Césaire's assertion that "At the end of formal humanism and philosophic renunciation, there is Hitler"? This poignant humanist (Pinn)/antihumanist (Césaire) tension, I contend, is at the heart of Wright's *Outsider*.[7]

"The question summed itself up: What's a man?"

Richard Wright, *The Outsider*

Cross Damon, the very complicated and ambiguous hero of *The Outsider*, enters into a conversation with the New York City district attorney, Ely Houston, about the nature of the human. During this conversation, Damon suggests that the human is an indefinable being: "'Maybe man is nothing in particular,' Cross said gropingly. 'Maybe that's the terror of it. Man may be just anything at all'" (172). Yoshinobu Hakutani interprets Damon's remarks as an instance of a "nihilistic view of the world" (172).[8] According to this view, because the human is not definable in a traditional sense, it is nothing, a useless passion, a vacuous blip waiting for extinction. But such a nihilistic interpretation does not ring true if we examine the subtle logic of Damon's claim.

The problem, according to Damon, is not that the human *is* definable as nothing; the problem is that the human, which so consistently resists being reduced to any specific conceptual system, "may be just anything at all." In other words, the human is a pluralistic being that can be defined in any number of ways, but can never be reduced to any single or ultimate definition, a view that is consistent with Fanon's philosophy of the human as a living rhythm. Damon's observation reflects an understanding of what Wolfgang Iser refers to as the shift from a mimetic to a performative theory of representation, a shift that has made it impossible to define the human. According to the performative view, literature, which Iser credits with having discovered the indefinability of the human, functions to expose not what the human is but the many shapes that the human can and does take: "Staging in literature makes conceivable the extraordinary plasticity of human beings, who, precisely because they do not seem to have a determinable nature, can expand into an almost unlimited range of culture-bound patternings. The impossibility of being present to ourselves becomes our possibility to play ourselves out to a fullness that knows no bounds, because no matter how vast the range, none of the possibilities will 'make us tick'" (297). When Damon claims that the human "may be just anything at all," he is not adopting a nihilistic worldview, as Hakutani suggests, but rather he is accepting the view that there can be many conceptual systems for signifying the human. Indeed, Hakutani concedes that, while Cross is a nihilist in the first half of the novel, he adopts a "conciliatory vision" (172) in the second half, a vision that is rooted in social justice and political freedom. My argument, however, is that Cross is never a nihilist; he is an unconditional honest atheist, as Nietzsche refers to the intellectually consistent nontheist, which implies a non nihilistic view of the human.

Throughout the novel, there are references not just to atheism but to genuine atheism. Cross first introduces the idea when discussing the nonobjective painting of Eva Blount, the wife of communist leader Gilbert Blount and the woman with whom Cross falls in love. According to Cross, "'Modern consciousness is Godlessness and nonobjective painting reflects this negatively.'" Not quite content with this description, Cross qualifies his claim by underscoring his view of total atheism: "'I mean Godlessness in a strict sense'" (274). Cross introduces this idea again in a discussion of the central ideas of modernism: "All of this brings us to one central, decisive fact: the consequences of the atheistic position of modern man" (482). Much later in the novel, Houston actually likens Cross to "real atheists" (564).

Atheism entails more than just a simple denial of God's existence so, when Cross and Houston refer to real or genuine atheists, their claim has serious implications. In "A Preface to Transgression," Michel Foucault argues, "The death of God is not merely an 'event' that gave shape to contemporary culture as we now know it; it continues tracing indefinitely its great skeletal outline"

(32). Genuine atheism does not occur in a single moment; it is a process in which the culture eliminates from its consciousness the ontotheological assumptions that continue to inform its intellectual systems despite the apparent absence of the God concept. This means that atheism in an early stage of development may not be considered atheism from a later perspective, that is, from a perspective when the "great skeletal outline" of atheism has become more clearly defined. In *Swann's Way*, for instance, Marcel Proust's narrator suggests that many nontheists remain theists by remaining committed to the theist's mind-set even though they have rejected God: even after "the death of the gods," the narrator says, "when a belief vanishes, there survives it . . . an idolatrous attachment to the old things which our faith in them did once animate" (324). To be a real atheist, Proust's narrator implies, the atheist must renounce not just God but also the "idolatrous attachment" to those things which faith once made real. Nietzsche makes a similar point in *The Gay Science* when he claims that, now that God is dead, "we still have to vanquish his shadow, too" (167).

Therefore, those who reject the God concept but still maintain a theological orientation toward the world would not qualify as genuine atheists. As for those who have shuffled off the mortal coils of belief, they frequently refer to themselves as thorough atheists. For instance, Freud calls himself not just an unbeliever but an "out-and-out unbeliever" (453). Virginia Woolf does not just deny the existence of God; she says that "certainly and emphatically there is no God" (72). Sartre makes a similar distinction when he shows how Enlightenment philosophers, while under the pretense of having abolished God from their philosophy, subscribe to a theological worldview by assuming that essence precedes existence, a view that presupposes the existence of a being who has spoken this essence into existence. As for Nietzsche, to be a genuine atheist, one must abandon the theological tradition's adherence to a metaphysical ideal: "Unconditional honest atheism (and *its* is the only air we breathe, we more spiritual men of this age!) is therefore *not* the antithesis of that ideal, as it appears to be; it is rather only one of the latest phases of its evolution, one of its terminal forms and inner consequences—it is the awe-inspiring *catastrophe* of two thousand years of training in truthfulness that finally forbids itself the *lie involved in belief in God*" (*Genealogy* 3.27). To be an unconditional honest atheist, one cannot merely be the exact opposite of the believer, for "the antithesis" of the believer's ideal is only a stage on the way to a genuine atheistic philosophy. And for Nietzsche, nihilists represent this antithesis, atheism in a stage of infancy if you will, which explains why he opposes nihilists as much as he opposes theists, a point he makes when he claims that the Übermensch will someday overcome both God and nothingness: "this Antichrist and antinihilist; this victor over God and nothingness—*he must come one day*" (*Genealogy* 2.24). God and nothingness are two sides of the same coin, and Nietzsche dispenses with the whole coin. More significantly, once the culture fully rejects God and nothingness and embraces unconditional honest atheism, there will be cause for rejoicing, for as Nietzsche claims, atheism means worldly redemption: "The concept 'God' has hitherto been the greatest objection to existence. . . . We deny God; in denying God, we deny accountability: only by doing *that* do we redeem the world" (*Twilight* 64).

Nietzsche and Cross reject nihilism because nihilists are actually closet theists in that they make use of a theological epistemology. According to an ontotheological system, God created individual beings through the power of the Word (Logos), which means that the Divine Word is one and the same as the object (referent) that God spoke into existence. Now that God no longer exists, according to many atheists, there has been a radical shift in our experience of language. Instead of subjecting the human (referent) to philosophical and biological analysis in order to determine its essential nature, unconditional honest atheists recognize that there is no ideal language to signify the human, because there is no God-realm from which the ideal language emanated. In his poem "Let There Be Light!" D. H. Lawrence articulates the consequences of this post-God mentality with admirable precision:

> If ever there was a beginning
> there was no god in it
> there was no Verb
> no Voice
> no Word.
>
> There was nothing to say:
> Let there be Light!
> All that story of Mr God switching on day
> is just conceit.
>
> Just man's conceit!
> —Who made the sun?
> —My child, I cannot tell a lie,
> I made it!

Complete Poems 681

The traditional view is that the world is like a sacred hieroglyph waiting to be correctly named. The task of the poet and philosopher, therefore, is to discover the pregiven language that best represents the world's essential nature. But if there is no God, then words could no longer serve their traditional function of incarnating the things they name. In other words, since there is no God, there can be no prediscursive Verb, no originary Voice, and above all, no Godly Word to describe the world. As Lawrence's narrator suggests, the theological discourse that pretends to describe the world as such "is just conceit," an egocentric human thought, a conceptual projection that enables humans to feel superior.

Understanding that all discourses are constructed explains the seemingly strange conclusion to Lawrence's poem. When the child asks who made the sun, the narrator replies that he did. At this point, the narrator does not mean that he has created that golden fireball blazing in the sky; he means the word *sun*, the human conceit that is used to signify the sun. Lawrence is clearly working within a Nietzschean tradition. In the "Truth and Lies" essay, when Nietzsche claims that truth is an illusion, there are two possible ways of interpreting this claim. According to the first, now that God is dead, there can be no truth that God spoke into being. Therefore, the belief in truth in an absolute sense is an illusion, a fable born in a more primitive age. According to this interpretation, truth does not exist. The second interpretation holds that language is a conceptual illusion (Nietzsche sometimes refers to this illusion as an innocent lie). The word *table* is not the same thing as the referent table, but for the sake of communication, humans must accept the word-illusion as a true representation of the referent table. Therefore, truth exists, but it exists as a conceptual illusion. Were there no language, the conceptual illusion would not exist. This second interpretation allows for truth assertions, so long as people bear in mind that the truth-claim is a personal and/or communal illusion, a provisional conceptual construct used for the sake of communication. When Lawrence's narrator says that he has created the sun, he is referring to the word-illusion *sun*, not to the referent sun.

Given the genuine atheist's view of concepts as a psychosemiotic construction instead of an ontological reality, it makes no sense to say that either God or nothingness is the essence of being. For unconditional honest atheists, all "ideas" are constructions, mere human inventions. Such atheists acknowledge and affirm the existence of tangible objects, but they do not acknowledge or affirm the existence of concepts that are best suited to represent objects. In terms of discourses used to signify the human, therefore, unconditional honest atheists would be disinclined to say that the human is essentially one thing or another. To quote Sartre: "Thus, there is no human nature, since there is not God to conceive it." But just because genuine atheists maintain an ironic distance from all discourses, it does not follow that they would dub the human essentially nothing. As Cross claims, the human is nothing in particular, because it can be any number of things.

"[T]he fact of the Third Reich alone makes obsolete forever any question of Christian superiority."

James Baldwin, *The Fire Next Time*

Wright ironically rejects the concept of the human, *not because it is (philosophically) impossible to narrate or define, but because it is too easy to (politically) narrate and define.* While those providing the narrative and definition of the human consider their discourses (in a philosophical sense) absolutely and essentially True, Wright considers them epistemic constructions of a communal will to power and dominance (in a political sense). At issue here, of course, is not what the human really is—such a question is unthinkable and absurd in Wright's genuinely atheistic world. Rather, the question is, What are the political consequences of adopting the view that there is such a thing as a true concept of the human? Wright details the horrific consequences through his depiction of communism and fascism, two movements that presuppose a theological orientation toward knowledge and the human, according to Wright.

Let me begin this section by detailing the theological presuppositions of fascism as depicted in the novel. Langley Herndon is the novel's open fascist, who also happens to be Gil Blount's landlord. As a communist, Blount wishes to provoke and eventually crush Herndon, so he invites Cross to board with him and his wife, Eva. A black man in a fascist-owned building will certainly infuriate Herndon—such is Blount's thinking. While Cross realizes that Blount is merely using him as a pawn in a political game, Cross accepts the challenge nonetheless, because he despises fascism slightly more than communism. What is significant for this analysis is the theological basis of Herndon's fascist philosophy.

There is a master race, a biologically superior people that has been specifically chosen to govern and rule biological inferiors. To persuade Cross to oppose Herndon and the fascists, Blount underscores this racist element in Herndon's philosophy: "He has the old-fashioned American racist notions, all of them, right up to the hilt, including the so-called biological inferiority of the Negro" (264). Herndon may have evolved a philosophy to justify his superior position in the body politic, but it is his theology that has enabled him to ground and control the epistemological/ontological recursive loop, for as Blount says of Herndon's view: "God made him [Herndon] and his kind to rule over the lower breeds" (264). Herndon, as a biological superior, knows the mind and will of God, and it is his God-ordained superiority that justifies his right "to rule over the lower breeds." If we consider Blount's depiction of Herndon's fascism in more detail, we will be able to better appreciate Césaire's claim that Hitler was no mere aberration in the West.

At this point, let me briefly detail the theistic basis of Hitler's political philosophy, for Herndon's ideas are clearly based on Hitler's theological worldview. In the year that Hitler came to power, he boldly declared his theological allegiance to Christianity: "[I]t is Christians and not international atheists who now stand at the head of Germany" ("Speech" 148). In *Mein Kampf*, Hitler articulated the Christian basis for his political vision, specifically insofar as it justified exterminating the Jews. In this text, Hitler concerns himself "with the spiritual nature of the people" (108). To his mind, Christians have assumed the new role of the chosen people, God's treasured possession. But to achieve their rightful place in the world, Hitler's chosen people, like Deuteronomy's holy elect, must degrade and destroy the spiritual cancer threatening the spiritual community. In the first part of *Mein Kampf*, Hitler sets the stage for his supersessionist project by mocking Jews as former possessors of the chosen people title. After discussing what Hitler claims to be the lack of hygiene in Jewish communities, he claims: "All this could scarcely be called very attractive; but it became positively repulsive when, in addition to their physical uncleanness, you discovered the moral stains on this 'chosen people'" (57). By asserting that Jews are physically and morally repugnant, Hitler implicitly exposes the absurdity of the Jewish claim to be chosen of God. Central to Hitler's view of Jews is his conviction that they are not and cannot be religious and therefore human in the true sense of the word: "[T]heir whole existence is based on one single great lie, to wit, that they are a religious community" (232). Indeed, Hitler explains that Jews, because they do not have a proper concept of the afterlife, cannot actually be spiritual beings: "Due to his own original special nature, the Jew cannot possess a religious institution, if for no other reason because he lacks idealism in any form, and hence belief in a hereafter is absolutely foreign to him. And a religion in the Aryan sense cannot be imagined which lacks the conviction of survival after death in some form. Indeed, the Talmud is not a book to prepare a man for the hereafter, but only for a practical and profitable life in this world" (306). Given the Jew's lack of spirituality, Hitler considers his or her "whole existence" as "an embodied protest against the aesthetics of the Lord's image" (178).

As a spiritual leader of the chosen people, Hitler believes that he has the obligation to construct a society that enables humanity to realize its highest spiritual destiny, that is, to reflect the image of God: "the task of preserving and advancing the highest humanity, given to this earth by the benevolence of the Almighty, seems truly a high mission" (398). Who establishes the criteria for determining humanness, much less "the highest humanity"? Who will decide which people have sufficiently met the criteria? Who will determine which people have failed to meet the minimum requirements? Since Hitler, as a spiritually chosen person, has a privileged relationship with the Divine, he is in the epistemological position to make such determinations. Indeed, it is incumbent upon him to do so, for as a political leader, he must have a clear definition in mind in order to enable his people to realize their highest humanity. Moreover, a clear definition is needed so that he can identify and expel all forces that would prohibit the potentially highest humans from realizing their destiny.

Because it is a theistic epistemology that enables Hitler to identify and define the highest humanity, he considers religion sacrosanct. Unfortunately, Hitler claims, through "the misuse of religion" (109) and "the abuse of Christianity" (268), Germany has not yet realized its true destiny, which is to establish a spiritual and holy community. For Hitler, "faith is often the sole foundation of a moral attitude" (267), so he considers the rejection of religion or God disastrous: "The attack against dogmas as such, therefore, strongly resembles the struggle against the general legal foundations of a state, and, as the latter would end in a total anarchy of the state, the former would end in a worthless religious nihilism" (267). To question God or His Truths could only lead to anarchy and nihilism, so Hitler, as a Catholic, encourages his reader to look to the Catholic Church for guidance in grounding its religious Truths: "Here, too, we can learn by the example of the Catholic Church. . . . It has recognized quite correctly that its power of resistance does not lie in its lesser or greater adaptation to the scientific findings of the moment, which in reality are always fluctuating, but rather in rigidly holding to dogmas once established, for it is only such dogmas which lend to the whole body the character of a faith" (459).[9] Solid, absolute, dogmatic Truth is the basis of a spiritual community, but this Truth can only come from God and religion: "Anyone who thinks he can arrive at a religious reformation by the detour of a political organization only shows that he has no glimmer of knowledge of the development of religious ideas or dogmas and their ecclesiastical consequences" (114). Given the primacy of religion, Hitler concludes, "*For the political leader the religious doctrines and institutions of his people must always remain inviolable*" (116).

Since challenging God's Truths would lead to anarchy and nihilism, Hitler makes it his task to purify the land of all those who do not follow the true teachings of Christ: "His [the Jew's] life is only of this world, and his spirit is inwardly alien to true Christianity as his nature two thousand years previous was to the great founder of the new doctrine. Of course, the latter made no secret of his attitude toward the Jewish people, and when necessary he even took to the whip to drive from the temple of the Lord this adversary of all humanity, who then as always saw in religion nothing but an instrument for his business existence" (307). The Jew focuses on things of this world, instead of basing his life on the spiritual principles of a religious dogma. For this reason, Hitler considers the Jew only a material creature, a being that fails to realize full humanity, much less "the highest humanity." But as the Bible suggests, just because nontheists refuse to believe, this does not justify exterminating them. The only way that Hitler could justify genocide to himself and others would be to demonstrate that the Jew threatens the spiritual life of the new chosen people. Such is the task he sets himself in *Mein Kampf*. In a passage that brings to mind Deuteronomy 20, Hitler explains why the Jew is so dangerous. Condemning the liberal writers of his time, whom he thinks to be Jewish, Hitler claims: "This was pestilence, spiritual pestilence, worse than the Black Death of olden times, and the people was being infected with it!" (58). The Black Death only destroyed human bodies, but "atheistic" Jews destroy the spiritual Christian community through their "Jewification of our spiritual life" (247). Given the spiritual corruption, Hitler considers the Jewish presence worse than the bubonic plague.[10] Such a logic leads Hitler to a reversal of the chosen people mentality. By referring to the Jews as a spiritual pestilence, Hitler suggests that their future destruction is a death sentence ordained by God: "For God's will gave men their form, their essence and their abilities. Anyone who destroys His work is declaring war on the Lord's creation, the Divine will. Therefore, let every man be active, each in his own denomination [Catholic or Protestant] if you please, and let every man take it as his first and most sacred duty to oppose anyone who in his activity by word or deed steps outside the confines of his religious community and tries to butt into the other" (562–63). God does not just call the chosen people; he calls the nonchosen to their own destruction, and since the chosen people are God's ministers of justice on earth, it falls upon them to enact God's will. Given Hitler's logic, if the chosen people want to keep the holy body of Christ intact, they must oppose the devilish enemy and, in a mighty struggle, hurl the heaven-storming Jew "back to Lucifer" (662). At this point, the Christian has, for Hitler, completely superseded the Jew. Whereas the Jews were once chosen as God's treasured possession, they are now chosen as a spiritual pestilence, the worshippers of false Gods who are to be genocidally destroyed. Thus explains Hitler's mission: "Hence today I believe that I am acting in accordance with the will of the Almighty Creator: *by defending myself against the Jew, I am fighting for the work of the Lord*" (65).

What is shocking about Wright's depiction of fascism is not the suggestion that it has a Christian and humanist basis, but that it inhabits the American mind generally, a view that Langston Hughes, James Baldwin, and Zora Neale Hurston share. Using Césaire's logic we could say that what Hitler has done to Jews in Europe, Americans have done to minorities in America. That Americans have not systematically and effectively coordinated their efforts as much as Hitler does not mean that they have adopted a more inclusive political system; it just means that the sociopolitical conditions were not ripe for Americans to follow through with its highest-humanity philosophy to its logical end. But African Americans have been able to expose the *dehumanizing* structures of western humanism. For instance, in a conversation at a local bar, Cross and his friends meet a tall man who voices what many minorities have experienced in America for centuries: "For four hundred years these white folks done made everybody on earth feel like they ain't human" (34). What has specifically enabled white folk to justify this subhuman view of certain minorities is their control of the God concept: "What's a black man to a white man? An ape made by God to cut wood and draw water, and with an inborn yen to rape white girls. . . . A Jew? A Christ-killer, a cheat, a rat" (35). Here we return to the epistemological/ontological recursive loop that has been used to justify marginalizing and violating so many groups of people. Since white people are, as Herndon claims, biological superiors, they can know the mind and will of God, and of course God tells the white person that he or she is superior and that the minority is subhuman (an ape or a rat). Blacks and Jews may want to question and challenge the white folks' representation of them as subhuman, but given their animal natures, they do not possess the spiritual faculty that would enable them to know the mind and will of God—as full-fledged material beings, apes and rats cannot have knowledge of spiritual realities. While Hitler and Herndon may be the only ones who overtly express their view of the minority as subhuman, this fascist ideology pervades American culture, as the tall man indicates and his auditors confirm. Wright suggests, as does Césaire, that Hitler's white-centered Christian humanism is the basis for defining American minorities as nonhuman, which explains why Herndon "Welcomed Hitler and publicly lauded his extermination of the Jews. Said that America should use the Negro as a scapegoat around which to unify the nation" (354). For Herndon, Hitler's highest-humanity philosophy is already in place in America; all that is needed now is a flag-waving cause to mobilize the masses: "The Negro was America's ace in the hole if the nation ever experienced any real internal stress. You could say that the nigger was the cause of it and get the rest of the nation to forget its problems and unite to get rid of the niggers" (355).

The common structure of mind that is behind Hitler's and Herndon's dehumanizing humanist philosophy is epistemological certitude with regard to the human, the kind of knowledge that the God concept functions to authorize and legitimize—"God made him and his kind to rule over the lower breeds." To distinguish "his kind" from "lower breeds," Herndon must have a clear and distinct idea of the various human and nonhuman gradations. Cross takes note of this mentality, for he claims that "Herndon's world considered him half-human" (334). German and American fascists represent the "highest humanity," while Jews and blacks represent the "lower breeds," and this is the case because God has created and ordered the world as such. Implicit in this particular view are the following assumptions. Human beings possess a distinct nature, which has been created by God for a specific purpose. Both God and his creation are *essentially* knowable, but only to those people who have a spiritual faculty of perception—in other words, those who have realized their "highest humanity." For those divinely chosen humans, either God created them with a superior epistemological faculty that enables them to see what the subhuman cannot or God specifically communicated spiritual ideas to his chosen few.

According to Cross, the type of knowledge that highest-humanity humanists claim to exist and have, however, is actually an epistemic construction of the will instead of a neutral and objective representation of the intellect. Following Nietzsche, Cross acknowledges the existence of mind-independent objects, but he categorically denies the existence of objective, neutral concepts that can signify or represent objects aright. Knowledge, language, and concepts are human inventions, necessary fictions that are the products of individual and communal desires for control. Such a view does not render language and concepts useless. It just means that they will reflect the interests, desires, and ideology of those who control the intellectual means of production.

This view of knowledge is for Cross, as it is for Nietzsche and Sartre, a direct consequence of his unconditional honest atheism. Cross states this explicitly in his conversation with Eva about nonobjective art. After emphatically declaring that modern consciousness is "Godlessness in a strict sense," Cross briefly outlines the consequences of this view of knowledge. The external world (mind-independent objects) exists, but since there "is nothing but *us, man,* and the world that *man* has made" (274), there can be no mind-independent language or concept that best reflects the world's essence or nature. For Cross, "What there is of the natural world that seems human to us is what we have projected out upon it from our own hearts" (274). Put differently, the conceptual systems that we have and use to systematize and order our experience of the mind-independent objects in the world emanate from the human instead of the mind-independent objects. Cross is clearly working within a Nietzschean tradition. Knowledge systems are culturally constructed and legitimated instruments of power and domination, and once a system takes possession of a person from within, the individual cannot help but perceive the world through that system: "Once a thorough system of sensual power as a way of life had gotten hold of a man's heart to the extent that it ordered and defined all of his relations, it was bound to codify and arrange all of his life's activities into one organic unity" (269). The system, a human construction, is what humans use to order and define the external world. While most people consider their conceptual system to be reality, Cross, again like Nietzsche, considers it to be an anthropomorphic construction, a conceptual will to power that assumes a provisional form in and through language. As a genuine atheist, therefore, Cross thinks it best to admit that all conceptual systems are individual and cultural constructions, which explains why he favors nonobjective art: since "the world we see is the world we make by our manual or emotional projection, why not let us be honest and paint our own projections, our fantasies, our own moods, our own conceptions of what things are" (275). Since all conceptual systems reflect human bias, let art at least honestly acknowledge that bias.

What differentiates atheists like Cross from theists like Herndon is their relationship to knowledge. Theists believe their conceptual system is a God-created reality, and not an anthropomorphic projection, that accurately reflects the world's essence, while unconditional honest atheists believe their conceptual system is a psychosemiotic construction, and not a God-created reality, that reflects human biases. Important for Wright is not so much that theists necessarily misrepresent the world, but that their system ultimately functions to divest the culturally marginalized of agency and control over their bodies and lives. Let me turn to Hitler once again to illustrate the devastating political consequences of this theistic position, for it is Hitler who is the basis for Herndon's character.

The black person is "a born half-ape," and while petty-bourgeois newspapers feature stories of black people becoming "a lawyer, teacher, even a pastor," this does not justify the "theory about the *equality of man*." Indeed, the "depraved bourgeois world" (430) fails to understand how training the "lower breeds" for the elite professions is actually "a sin against all reason" and God: "it is criminal lunacy to keep on drilling a born half-ape until people think they have made a lawyer out of him, while millions of members of the highest culture-race must remain in entirely unworthy positions; . . . it is a sin against the will of the Eternal Creator if His most gifted beings by the hundreds and hundreds of thousands are allowed to degenerate in the present proletarian morass, while Hottentots and Zulu Kaffirs are trained for intellectual professions" (Hitler, *Mein Kampf* 430). While the bourgeois world may think that it is educating black folk by teaching them to enter the intellectual professions, what it is actually giving them "is training exactly like that of the poodle, and not scientific 'education'" (430). This is the case because black people are by nature more animal than human. White people can understand the foundational and governing principles of a conceptual system, while black people can only do what the conceptual system orders them to do. Given this ontological difference, black people can never actually be educated in the true sense of the word, which is why Hitler claims that training them for the intellectual professions resembles the training of a poodle. Since only God's "most gifted beings" have the intellectual capacity to understand the theoretical and philosophical basis of a conceptual system, it is imperative that they remain in professional positions of authority to maintain a stable and well-functioning society.

Hitler's theistic relationship to knowledge divests black people of agency and control over their bodies and lives on two levels. First, by defining people of African descent as intellectually defective, he justifies to himself and others his claim that blacks should not and cannot be in professional positions of authority. Defective in reason, blacks are not as fully human as whites, so whites must assume the role of governing and ruling nonwhites. Second, by virtue of his ontological superiority as a full-fledged human, Hitler is in an epistemological position to define what constitutes the human and to determine who meets the minimum requirements of the definition. Given his epistemological superiority, even if Hitler were to claim that blacks are fully human, his act of defining them as such would implicitly place him on a higher ontological level than people of African descent. It would, as Fanon and Redding argue, implicitly divest blacks of the ability and freedom to participate in the process of self-formation and self-definition. *For Wright, these two functions of the God concept are the essence of theism*, so if someone approaches knowledge as do Hitler and Herndon, they would be theists, even if they proclaimed themselves atheists. And indeed, in *The Outsider*, it is the communists who are theists without God, for their relationship to knowledge functions to divest culturally marginalized figures of power over their individual bodies.

"The only trouble was that he and his kind were restlessly envious of the priests, the churches, the Communists, the Fascists, the men of power."

Richard Wright, *The Outsider*

Wright does not object to fascism or communism so much as to their basis in a political project of "total power" (328), a project that begins with a theistic orientation toward knowledge. Practitioners of each system presuppose, according to Wright, the existence of one way, one truth, and one life, and given their privileged epistemological position in the world, they are best stationed to determine that one way, that single truth, and that true life. But for Cross, all conceptual systems about the world are exactly that: systems ("our own conceptions of what things are") that humans project upon the world to systematize and order one's experiences. They are not ontological realities waiting to be discovered. Of course, those who create a system of "total power" will brook no alternative system, so they will do whatever is necessary to consolidate their power and to crush dissenters. Cross begins to understand precisely how this closed system of power functions through his interactions with communists like Jack Hilton and Gil Blount, who subscribe to different truths than fascists and theists, but who have a similar basis in a system of "total power." This is most readily seen when Hilton and Blount *dehuman-*

ize and *demoralize* Bob Hunter, a porter whom Cross meets on a train from Chicago to New York.

Bob is a significant figure in the novel because he is insignificant; he represents the everyday marginalized person who is divested of autonomy and control over his individual body and life by those who wield a system of "total power." Initially, the Party assigns him the task of organizing cells in the Dining Car Waiters' Union, but when Bob introduces Cross to Hilton and Blount for the first time, Hilton informs Bob that he must stop organizing. As a relatively intelligent man who has been working "night and day" (245) to organize and recruit for the Party, Bob pleads his case. But Hilton does not relent. Because Bob persists, at the behest of his wife, Sarah, the Party informs immigration that Bob is an illegal alien. He is then deported to Trinidad, where he will be imprisoned and die as a political dissenter. Later in the novel, when Cross challenges Hilton's actions, Hilton responds: "'There are a million Bob Hunters. What do they mean? What do they count?'" (399). While Cross and Sarah consider Bob human, Cross realizes that he is not human according to the Communist Party leaders: "To Hilton, Bob was only something to be sacrificed in the interests of a vast design" (448). In essence, the Party turns everyday people like Bob "into an object, a thing, a means" (460).

The Party achieves this objective by using the same theistic epistemology as the fascists. Cross begins to understand this theistic system when Hilton upbraids Bob. Hilton's "high pitch of oratory" is excessive, but Cross senses that the message has been delivered in such a manner in "an attempt to impose a respect for higher authority" (245). Positing the existence of a "higher authority" is absolutely necessary, for as Edward Said rightly observes, knowledge that is seen as politically or ideologically constructed is not considered true knowledge in the West. In other words, without the existence of a transhuman "higher authority," one would have to acknowledge that all concepts are human constructed rather than mind-independent, which would radically undermine the western myth of neutral and objective knowledge. In terms of an established hierarchy ranging from the full-fledged human to the half-human or subhuman, only those who have attained the highest humanity would be in a position to have true knowledge. In concrete terms, this means that Hilton, who has achieved a higher humanity than Bob, has epistemological access to this "higher authority." So when Hilton opposes Bob, it is not Hilton's personal desire for power that has dictated his comments; it is the "higher authority." For everyday underlings like Bob, understanding this "higher authority" is not necessary; only obedience is (246). As Gil says to Bob: "'You are an instrument of the Party. You exist to execute the Party's will. That's all there is to it'" (248). Obviously, Hilton and Gil, as full-fledged humans, have the power and ability to understand this "higher authority," which places them firmly above lackeys like Bob, just as Herndon and Hitler have the power and ability to understand Divine mandates, which places them firmly above the "lower breeds."

Fascists and communists exude an epistemological certitude that is extremely seductive. What makes communism so enticing is "its believing that it *knew* life; its *conviction* that it has mastered the act of living; its *will* that it could define the ends of existence that fascinated him against his volition" (255). Communists, like fascists, believe that they know life, have a conviction that they have mastered living, and desire to define the aims of existence, and while Cross knows that their knowledge, conviction, and will are projections of their own desire for power instead of realities, he feels the lure of such certitude. After all, such certitude is the perfect instrument for obtaining total power over others.

But Cross is too intelligent to be duped by any such system. As an unconditional honest atheist, Cross exposes fascist and communist systems as closed wills to power and dominance. After a conversation with Gil, Cross starts to understand what the closed system of absolute power entails: "To hold absolute power over others, to define what they should love or fear, to decide if they were to live or die and thereby to ravage the whole of their beings—that was a sensuality that made sexual passion look pale by comparison" (267). Hilton and Blount subscribe to a communist "conception of existence," but what really motivates them, according to Cross, is "absolute power over others," and it is their conceptual system that enables them to enact such power. On the basis of their privileged access to the "higher authority," they are in a position to "define" and "decide"—they can define who is human and who is not, and they can decide what role, if any, individuals can play in the Party's "vast design."

For Cross, of course, there is no "higher authority" that authorizes and legitimizes the existence of a transhuman objective concept. All concepts are psychosemiotic constructions ("our own conceptions of what things are"). But there is a palpable difference between individuals who wield an absolute rather than a provisional will to power. Those who seek "total power" are total sadists. As Cross claims, "It was power" that these men wanted, "not just the exercise of bureaucratic control, but personal power to be wielded directly upon the lives and bodies of others. He recalled how Hilton and Gil had looked at Bob when Bob had pled against the Party's decision. They had enjoyed it, loved it!" (267) Gil and Hilton create the illusion that there is a "higher authority" that not only justifies but also necessitates their actions, but Cross realizes that the idea of the "higher authority" is simply a legitimizing concept; it is an idea that allows people like Gil and Hilton to wield "personal power . . . directly upon the lives and bodies of others" with impunity. Significantly, there is a joy attached to this act of degrading, violating, and dominating others. The more Gil and Hilton demoralize and dehumanize Bob, the more secure is their system of power and therefore their humanity, for it is only the highest humans who possess the requisite knowledge and authority to wield the total system of power. In essence, the more Gil and Hilton *dehumanize* Bob, the more they *humanize* themselves, and since personal gratification comes from consolidating one's power through becoming human, *dehumanizing* others increases one's enjoyment—hence, Gil and Hilton's sadism.

While the other characters in the novel, with the exception of Houston, are neither attentive nor astute enough to process how such systems ultimately dehumanize, Cross does understand, which leads him to a violent counter-dehumanizing reaction. For instance, early in the novel, when a couple of people are discussing Cross, he feels "deprived of his humanity, converted into a condemned object" (47). For Cross, to be human is to have agency, control over one's body and life, so when others take epistemic control of his body, Cross loses his sense of autonomy and feels like "a condemned object," a lifeless thing that is named into being. Making Cross feel this way, however, is dangerous, for when he first meets the communists, he feels that they are outsiders, like himself. But after he starts to recognize how their sadistic humanist philosophy dehumanizes others, he senses within himself the desire to retaliate in like manner: "He could have waved his hand and blotted them from existence with no more regret of taking human lives than if he had swatted a couple of insects. Why could he never make others realize how dangerous it was for them to make him feel like this?" (232). Gil and Hilton never say that Cross is less than human. But because they control the epistemological/ontological recursive loop (given their privileged knowledge of the "higher authority," they are in a position to "define" and "decide" the fate of others), they implicitly act as if they are more human than Cross—they have a superior intellectual capacity, which gives them the right to rule and govern others. Since Cross refuses to allow himself to be dehumanized, he responds by dehumanizing them—he assumes a superior intellectual posture, which gives him the right to rule and govern them, acts that implicitly convert Hilton and Gil into objects. If they are going to implicitly act more human by defining and deciding his being and fate, then he will recover his humanity by defining and deciding their being and fate.

Such a response to the system of total power, however, is ultimately destructive. Cross realizes this after he kills Gil and Herndon: "[I]f you fought men who tried to conquer you in terms of total power you too had to use total power and in the end you became what you tried to defeat" (328). Cross's fatal flaw is his highest-humanity posturing, the same posturing that has been central to the way the fascists and communists treat others, according to Wright. The problem is this: to fight the system of total power, which ultimately infects all those involved ("their disease had reached out and claimed him too" [309]), he must assume the posture of being more human than Gil and Hilton, the very posture that he has denounced because it makes him feel less than human. Let me put this differently. The fascist claims that life is X, while the communist claims that life is not X, but Y. Both know what life essentially is because they have superior intellectual capacities, which gives them the right to rule and govern others. To challenge the fascists and communists, Cross must pretend to have a superior intellectual capacity, which would give him the right to rule and govern others (that is, life is not essentially X or Y, but Z, and Cross is epistemologically stationed to know this with certainty, because he is a full-fledged human). Once the system of total power, which presupposes the idea of a fully realized human, is set into motion, the only way to oppose it is to implicitly appropriate a system of total or absolute power. And since this system is based on a highest-humanity philosophy, those who do not understand or accept it will be implicitly downgraded in the hierarchical chain of human beings—and some will even be converted into animals or things.

For Wright, all of these systems are based on a theological model of knowledge, which explains why he has Cross liken communism to Christianity. For instance, after interacting with a Party member, "Cross found himself paraphrasing a Biblical passage": "*Thou shalt not depend upon others, nor trust them: for this your Party is a jealous Party, visiting the suspicions of the leaders upon the members unto the third and fourth friends of the friends around the Party*" (461). Communism and Christianity may have different "truths," but they are both based on a similar model of total and absolute power, a model that begins with an act of epistemological certitude. Cross does not have such certitude, which is why he envies "the priests, the churches, the Communists, the Fascists, the men of power" (555). Were he able to act as if he were in possession of the one Way, the absolute Truth, and the only Life, he would be able to reap the benefits, which would primarily be the freedom to wield a system of total power. But he knows that the Truth that all these autocratic systems have been based on are ruthless wills to power and dominance rather than God-created objective Truths (the "higher authority"), so he cannot justify acting like one of "the men of power."

Given the way that all these systems are grounded on epistemological certitude with regard to a concept, were humanism to lay epistemological claim to the true definition of the human or human nature, it would implicitly become a profoundly dehumanizing philosophy, for all those people who would not accept the humanist's definition of the true human would have implicitly failed to realize their highest humanity. This is the reason why Césaire and Lyotard are so critical of humanism. While humanism is a philosophy that purports to improve the quality of human living, it has been, all too often, a system that has consistently dehumanized many people. Therefore, it is in the name of social equality that antihumanists oppose humanism.

"Man is a promise that he must never break."
Richard Wright, *The Outsider*

A friend of Césaire's and in the intellectual tradition of Lyotard, Wright certainly understood the dehumanizing impulse at the heart of humanism. And yet Wright was a self-avowed humanist nonetheless.[11] To understand his distinct brand of humanism, we must work through the logic of his unconditional honest atheism, a vision he shares with Cross.

According to Cross, theists believe that there exists not only mind-independent objects but also concepts that are best equipped to signify and represent objects. Given the theist's epistemological superiority, they are best stationed to know with certainty the nature of a specific concept, like the human. But for Cross, Godlessness in a strict sense means that all concepts are human inventions, mental projections that assume a provisional form in and through a semiotic sign. To say what the human is in and of itself, therefore, would be an incoherent proposition, according to Cross. This is the case because ideas are nothing more than "our own conceptions of what things are." Since ideas are human constructed rather than ontologically pregiven, Cross can only cast a skeptical glance on all ideas, for he knows that all humans will construct concepts in relation to their own cultural contexts and ideological needs and desires. It is this ironic distance from ideas that makes Cross resist submitting to any single party or -ism: "For Cross had no party, no myths, no tradition, no race, no soil, no culture, and no ideas—except perhaps the idea that ideas in themselves were, at best, dubious!" (504–5). Cross could never be a classical humanist, because to do so, he must affirm the existence of a pregiven idea like the human or humanism. But since Cross, like Nietzsche and Sartre, rejects the idea of a mind-independent concept, he looks at ideas as human constructs, which means that, were he to accept an idea like the human or humanism, it would be as a human-constructed idea instead of as a conceptual reality.

While Cross refuses to submit to any party or idea, it does not follow that he rejects humanism altogether. It just means that he rejects a metaphysical humanism, a pregiven ontological humanism that is predicated on an absolute understanding of human nature.[12] Cross discloses his commitment to humanism in the closing moments of the novel, just after he has been fatally shot. In his final conversation with Houston, Cross says: "Alone a man is nothing. . . . Man is a promise that he must never break" (585). By calling the human a "promise," Cross brilliantly revises humanism. According to classical humanism, the objective has been to define the human in its ideal form, to identify who has realized his or her highest humanity, to civilize those subhuman cultures that have not yet understood what it means to be truly human, and to stratify culture on the basis of the various gradations of humanness and subhumanness. Cross's humanism is original because he bases it on a socially constructed promise rather than a human nature.

Given the way human nature–based humanist philosophies have dehumanized so many, it might seem that all Cross would have to do to establish a more socially just humanism would be to create a more inclusive definition of human nature. But Cross realizes that the "men of power" would ultimately manipulate whatever definition that has been created in order to justify categorizing some people as members of the "lower breeds." After all, Cross is much more intelligent than all the fascists and communists in the novel, but that does not stop them from treating him as subhuman. Therefore, Cross realizes that he must create a humanism that is not based on a superior epistemological capacity or a human nature. Cross finds his answer in a humanism that is based on a promise. A promise is an agreement, a social contract of sorts. As a genuine atheist, Cross would not accept the traditional view that humans have an inherent dignity, so he would not admonish others to respect humans because humans are essentially sacred and inviolable beings. To understand the necessity of rejecting the inherent dignity of the human, let me contrast Heidegger and Cross. Heidegger rejects humanism because "the highest determinations of the essence of man in humanism still do not realize the proper dignity of man" (210). Notice how Heidegger's claim implies an inherent dignity that humanists have failed to see or understand. With a proper epistemology, Heidegger's logic suggests, humanists would be able to know what the true and proper dignity of the human is. But alas, humanists, who are epistemologically inferior according to Heidegger, look but do not see, listen but do not hear. Heidegger's condemnation of humanism is based on the epistemological/ontological recursive loop of theology, which implicitly elevates Heidegger and demotes classical humanists in the scale of human being. Given Heidegger's epistemological superiority, he can see "the *humanitas* of man" (210) at its highest point, which implies, of course, that Heidegger has understood or experienced this highest humanity. And for those who have failed to experience Heidegger's "*humanitas* of man," we can infer that they have not realized their highest humanity.

For an unconditional honest atheist, like Cross, there can be no proper dignity of the human, for there is no force or being that authorizes or legitimizes such a dignity. So instead of claiming that humans have a proper dignity, which he is in a privileged epistemological position to see and understand, Cross pleads with others to make a social agreement to treat the human as a promise that should not be broken. In a certain sense, Cross does not differ substantially from Heidegger in *what* he says—they both claim that humans should be treated with dignity and respect. But the two differ totally in *how* they speak. Heidegger's way of speaking implies a gradation of human being, and since he is epistemologically superior (fully human), we can infer that he has a proper grasp of the highest "*humanitas* of man." By contrast, Cross's way of speaking does not imply an epistemological superiority. He wants others to treat the human as a promise, an "idea" that has promise only insofar as the promise of the human is kept. Cross's intellectual move at this point is brilliant because in considering the human a promise, he avoids the stratification of humanness that is implied in the epistemological/ontological recursive loop.

In a strange way, we could say that the doctrine of the inherent dignity of the human is what leads to the dehumanization of many humans, because those who claim to have epistemological access to the concept of humanity's inherent dignity implicitly elevate themselves and demote nonknowers in the hierarchical chain of human being. To be more precise, since the epistemologically privileged can see what others cannot, they must be ontologically

superior, and therefore fully human, while those who have not yet compre-
hended the human's inherent dignity must be ontologically inferior and therefore not fully human. And as Césaire and Lyotard argue, once humanists claim
to know the proper dignity of the human, they are only one step away from
implementing a dehumanizing project of humanizing those who have failed
to interiorize the true concept of humanness. Such is the basis of Césaire's
claim that humanism has justified colonization and, taken to its logical end,
ultimately Hitler.

It is this dehumanizing impulse at the heart of humanism that leads Cross
to reject a metaphysical humanism in favor of a constructed humanism. Indeed, genuine atheists, like Cross, who abandon the idea of humanity's inherent dignity, make a truly egalitarian and democratic experience of culture
possible, because their way of talking invites and thereby empowers others to
engage in the process of constructing a socially agreed upon promise, like the
human. Heidegger's way of talking implies true, pregiven "ideas" that can be
known and that he is best stationed to know (the human has a proper dignity,
and as a full-fledged human, he can know this proper dignity), while Cross's
way of talking implies communal participation and negotiation in the social
construction of ideas like the human or human dignity (he implicitly invites
others to participate in the construction of the human as a promise that cannot be broken). As should be clear by this point, Heidegger's vision of the
human is based on a true understanding of something inherent within the
human, and only those who adopt an epistemology similar to his can know
and understand this something, while Cross's vision is based on a socially
constructed agreement. This constructionist orientation toward knowledge
does not presuppose a stratification of humanness. Cross does not say that the
human has an inherent essence that he is best epistemologically stationed to
know; instead, he invites others to treat the human as an inviolable promise.
His very act of working together with others to construct a concept of the
human empowers all those who participate in this construction of the idea of
the human as a promise.

The distinctive feature of Cross's humanism is its basis in establishing a
democratic and egalitarian connection between humans. As Cross claims, his
goal is "[t]o make a bridge from man to man" (585). The humanisms in the
West may have built bridges between one epistemologically superior white
man and another, but they have ultimately put up walls between themselves
and women, Africans, Native Americans, Jews, and many others through their
posturing as epistemological and hence ontological superiors. The problem is

this: even if metaphysical humanists were to claim that all humans possess an inherent dignity, the very act of making this claim functions to dehumanize others. More specifically, because white men are epistemologically superior, they can determine and define others, acts that implicitly elevate them and demote nonknowers and nondefiners in the scale of human beings. In essence, the whole western apparatus of knowable and discoverable Ideas sets into motion a political system that presupposes the full-fledged humanness of certain people and the subhumanness of others. For those who have access to true, pregiven Ideas, we can conclude that they are fully human, whereas for those who do not have access, we can conclude that they are not. Relying on this distinction, whether they have known it or not, whether they have intended it or not, humanists have justified a political system that ultimately divests certain people of the freedom to participate in the construction of themselves as humans. The apparatus of knowable and discoverable ideas implicitly makes an egalitarian and democratic body politic impossible.

For Cross, the first step toward building bridges between humans is to reject the idea of a knowable human essence or dignity; in his world, all knowledge is socially constructed. This does not mean that he sees the human as a being with no dignity—neither Cross nor Wright were nihilists. It just means that he wishes to construct the human as a being with promise. This approach avoids the dehumanizing impulse because it resists claiming that any one person has a superior epistemological capacity. By adopting this view that knowledge is communally constructed rather than ontologically pregiven, Cross shifts the focus from knowledge as individual discovery (a system that implicitly stratifies humanness on the basis of a person's epistemological capacity) to knowledge as social construction (a system that implicitly rejects the idea of knowledge as essentially discoverable and thereby avoids the stratification of humanness implicit in the epistemological/ontological recursive loop). According to this view, there can be no true or final knowledge. Moreover, for socially constructed knowledge to be truly egalitarian and democratic, all people must be invited to participate in its construction.

Understanding Cross's view of knowledge as human constructed explains his concluding remark: "I'm *innocent*" (586). Certainly, as readers, we must ask how he can justify such a claim. After all, he has abandoned his family, gotten a minor pregnant, and killed four people. To call himself innocent verges on the offensive if not the absurd. And yet, given the logic of *The Outsider*, living in a political system that is based on the epistemological/ontological recursive loop of theology divests significant numbers of people of individual agency and personal freedom. Cross is innocent because, as a genuine atheist, he never subscribed to the view that there exists a mind-independent concept that he is in a privileged epistemological position to know. But as a black man living in a racist society that grounds its politics on the epistemological/ontological recursive loop of theology, he can never create himself as human. For instance, even when the communists welcome Cross into their system with a surface rhetoric of equality, their way of talking and method of interacting with him functions to dehumanize him. To create a truly egalitarian and democratic system of living, to build bridges between all people, Cross suggests that the culture must totally reconfigure knowledge as social construction. That means it must adopt a totally godless view of knowledge. And until the culture accepts such an approach, democracy will not be possible and retaliatory violence will be the norm.

To return to the question about humanism as "a grounding for liberative action within African American history" (Pinn) versus the idea that humanism leads to Hitler (Césaire), we could say that both of these claims are right. So long as humanism is based on a pregiven idea, especially a concept of human nature, humanness will be stratified in relation to an individual's capacity to know that nature. From the perspective of antihumanist intellectuals (like Césaire and Wright) who consider knowledge a political construction rather than a mind-independent concept, humanism has been and can be used to justify dubbing certain people subhuman or nonhuman, a naming act that vindicates aggressively intrusive and coercive political agendas. Antihumanists in this tradition do not reject humanism because inhuman systems compromise the semantic integrity of that animal most noble in reason. They reject humanism because the humanist's concept of the human is the most effective tool for constructing and justifying oppressive political systems. Those who have epistemological access to clear and distinct ideas about the human have obviously realized their "highest humanity" and are therefore in a position to define and decide, to rule and govern. Those who do not have a clear and distinct idea about the human have obviously failed to realize their "highest humanity" and therefore must be defined and ruled. Hitler's and Heidegger's approach to the human is precisely the mind-set that Césaire and Wright denounce.

But Hitler's and Heidegger's approach to the human cannot be reconciled with Cross's humanism as promise, because Hitler and Heidegger presuppose the existence of a mind-independent concept that they are uniquely situated to know. As Cross suggests, all concepts are "our own conception of what things are." In other words, ideas are human constructed, which means that they reflect the "power, position, and interests" (Said, *Humanism* 48) of those who construct them. Moreover, given the "subjective element in humanistic knowledge" (12), all knowledge systems will reflect human bias and limitations, so instead of treating knowledge systems as neutral, objective, and inviolable, humanists, like Said and Wright, treat knowledge as provisional, limited, subject to critique. I find Said extremely compelling at this point. Given our understanding of concepts as human-constructed, it is necessary to situate "critique at the very heart of humanism, critique as a form of democratic freedom and as a continuous practice of questioning and of accumulating knowledge" (47). No more dogmatic positing of the "highest humanity" or the "dignity proper" to the human but a humble acknowledgment that one's concept of the human as a construction is the mark of an internally consistent humanist. And with such an acknowledgment comes the necessity of critique, a critique that involves the Other's input, the Other's "power, position, and interests," the very things one may miss in the construction of one's own concept of what humans are. The humanist's construction of the human must take the form of a promise, a socially constructed agreement that has promise only insofar as the promise of the human is kept. Because Wright subscribes to such a view of humanism, his humanism is, as Pinn claims, "liberative."

3

No Means Yes

The Conversion Narrative as Rape Scene in Nella Larsen's *Quicksand*

"This business of saving souls had no ethics."
Richard Wright, *Black Boy*

In the 1928 novella *Quicksand*, Nella Larsen dramatizes the religious conversion as a gang rape. The blasphemy of this depiction would be gratuitous were the reader unaware of the indignities that African Americans have suffered because of belief in God. But keeping in mind Kabnis's declaration that God is ugly even though he does not exist, Redding's claim that God and the word of God have been used to perpetuate the wicked idea of human inferiority, Fanon's observation that belief is used to convert colonized infidels into animals, and Wright's contention that the God concept functions to divest culturally designated inferiors of human agency, Larsen's decision to use the metaphor of a gang rape to depict the unscrupulous tactics of believers for converting the infidel would be less offensive and more logical than one would initially assume.

Before I turn to the text, let me briefly provide a context for Larsen's depiction of believers as gang rapists. Important to note is that atheistic critics of faith are not the originators of such a blasphemous metaphor. In fact, God is depicted as a rapist in the Bible, specifically in Jeremiah. Because of Jerusalem's inability to be faithful to the Lord, God seeks a second Bride, which He finds in the reluctant prophet Jeremiah. Significantly, Jeremiah's depiction of his act of consent sounds like a date-rape, where the victim's no really means yes for the perpetrator. Here's how the crucial passage reads: "Yahweh, you seduced me unlawfully, and I consented to being seduced; you raped me, and you were too strong for my resistance to prevail" (Jeremiah 20:7).[1] As Abraham Heschel, James Crenshaw, and Harold Bloom have all observed of this passage, crucial are the verbs *patah*, which "refers to seducing 'a maid that is not betrothed' before or without marriage," and *chasack*, which "refers to sexual violence, and elsewhere to adulterous rape" (Bloom 15). What God has done to Jeremiah may seem, on the surface, unlawful, but from a spiritual perspective, which God understands much better than Jeremiah, God has given Jeremiah what his soul secretly desires, which is full communion with the Divine. So from a legal and secular perspective, God's rape of Jeremiah is a heinous crime, but from a spiritual perspective, the Lord's violent and imposing actions represent the best thing that could have happened (spiritual union), which explains why Jeremiah is ultimately grateful for being raped.

In "Batter my heart, three-personed God," John Donne intelligently teases out the logical implications of this rape metaphor, specifically underscoring the contradiction between the secular and spiritual laws of being. The narrator of this poem is "betrothed" to God's enemy, so the narrator asks God to "Divorce me, untie, or break that knot" which binds the unbeliever to the unholy one. Because the narrator is governed by worldly passion instead of Godly reason, he cannot live in accord with the spiritual laws of being. Indeed, the narrator considers himself a slave to secular desire. According to this view, the only way to be free would be to adopt a spiritual perspective of life, which would enable the narrator to overcome his enslavement to Satan, Sin, and Death. As with Jeremiah, rape is not only justified in order to awaken the narrator's deepest spiritual desires; it is absolutely necessary. As Donne's narrator concludes, he shall never "be free, / Nor ever chaste, / except you [God] ravish me" (314–15). From a spiritual perspective, rape, while something unlawful and to be resisted, is actually necessary and even desirable.

This spiritual justification of force and even rape lays the ground for a large-scale project of epistemic and psychological violence. From the believer's spiritual perspective, the most basic and secret desire of all humans is communion with the Divine. Since believers know God and His will, they can speak with authority not only about the general spiritual desire but also the individual destinies of all humans. Of course, erring infidels, who do not and cannot know their God-ordained destiny, pursue a lifestyle inconsistent with the spiritual laws of their own being. To use violence and/or force to compel the infidel to adopt a spiritual perspective, therefore, would not only be a God-sanctioned action; it would be a God-like act. Put differently, without a spiritual rape, it is possible that the infidel would fail to experience a spiritual rebirth, which would lead the infidel to remain in bondage to Satan and the world.

"I really mean that there was no love in the church. It was a mask for hatred and self-hatred and despair."

James Baldwin, *The Fire Next Time*

Quicksand traces the life journey of the curious, independent, and sexually frustrated Helga Crane, a restless woman who is searching for a place to call home, somewhere where she can cultivate meaningful relationships and be accorded dignity. To find such security, she journeys to Naxos, Chicago, New York, and Copenhagen, but having failed in each location, she finally enters a Harlem church where a congregation of believers is singing songs of worship. Significantly, the language here is sexually charged, as Deborah E. McDowell observes: "The sexual desires, pent-up throughout the novel, finally explode in Helga's primitive, passionate religious conversion, the description of which unambiguously simulates sexual excitement and orgasmic release" (xix–xx). Given these sexual references, McDowell claims that "Larsen dramatizes the fine line between sexual and religious ecstacy in fundamentalist religion" (xx). To my mind, however, the references are stronger than just sex; they suggest a rape, a detail that radically impacts the way we interpret the conversion scene. That Helga is forced against her will is clear from the language of possession throughout the scene, for everything in the chapter divests her of agency. For instance, by singing the hymn "Showers of Blessings," the community effectively instructs Helga in the art of renouncing her own personal desires, her selfish attachment to self, in order to make room for God. To achieve this objective, the believers sing slowly and carefully as the song strategically charts Helga's loss of individual identity. During the first part, the song details the selfish impulse to have a singular self, an act that directly excludes God:

Oh, the bitter shame and sorrow
That a time could ever be,
When I let the Savior's pity
Plead in vain, and proudly answered:
"All of self and none of Thee." (111)

As the song progresses, the self gives way to God until the Divine takes full possession of the individual: "Some of self and some of Thee" becomes "Less of self and more of Thee" (112). Though the believers do not utter what logically follows, the reader can infer that full possession means "none of self and all of Thee."

After the song comes to an end, the believers intensify their strategies of manipulation and coercion by strategically preventing Helga from thinking. To achieve this goal, the community must take possession of her, and to highlight the believers' intent to control and possess, the narrator makes use of a rhetoric of entrapment. For instance, when Helga initially breaks down, a woman "jumped up and down before Helga *clutching* at the girl's soaked coat." Still resistant at this point, "Helga had shrunk from her *grasp*," this "crazed creature's *hold*," but the faithful have no intention of letting her go free (my emphases 112). As the believers surround the scarlet woman, Helga feels repulsed by the whole affair, but somehow "the horror *held* her" (my emphasis 113). Finally, after succumbing to the insanity of this lurid experience, Helga feels "herself *possessed* by the same madness" (my emphasis 113). The rhetoric of entrapment—clutched, grasped, held, possessed—indicates that a force has taken control of Helga's body. Not surprisingly, just before Helga succumbs to belief, "she gathered herself for one last effort to escape" (113), but to no avail.

While it is important to note this language of entrapment, it is just as crucial to observe precisely when the believers crowd around Helga. At the conclusion of the song, Helga "gave herself freely to soothing tears, not noticing that the groaning and sobbing of those around her had increased" (112). No longer fully conscious, Helga lets her guard down until the "crazed woman" clutches her coat. At this point, Helga momentarily regains control of her senses: "Alarmed for the fraction of a second, involuntarily Helga had shrunk from her grasp" (112). Not surprisingly, having recovered her senses, Helga becomes the astute observer and critical thinker we have come to know in the first hundred pages: "Helga Crane was amused, angry, disdainful, as she sat there, listening to the preacher praying for her soul" (113). Sensing Helga's resistance, the believers intensify their entrapment strategies, and it is then that the discourse becomes overtly sexual: "She remained motionless, watching, as if she lacked the strength to leave the place—foul, vile, and terrible, with its mixture of breaths, its contact of bodies, its concerted convulsions, all in wild appeal for a single soul. Her soul" (113). During the group's orgasmic "convulsions," Helga finds herself paralyzed, terrified, and disgusted. Moreover, as the "contact of bodies" overwhelms her, the scene escalates into a rape scene: "And as Helga watched and listened, gradually a curious influence penetrated her; she felt an echo of the weird orgy resound in her own heart; she felt herself possessed by the same madness" (113). The contact of bodies and the orgasmic convulsions lead to penetration ("penetrated her"), a "weird orgy" in which Helga is the sexual object of desire. Not surprisingly, the religious moment climaxes with the women behaving "like reptiles, sobbing and pulling their hair and tearing off their clothing" (114).

If my depiction of this scene has been convincing, that the conversion is described in terms of a gang rape, the conclusion of the chapter can only take the reader by surprise, for in a sudden moment, Helga undergoes a radical transformation: "A miraculous calm came upon her. Life seemed to expand, and to become very easy. Helga Crane felt within her a supreme aspiration toward the regaining of simple happiness, a happiness unburdened by the complexities of the lives she had known" (114). As readers who have any sensitivity for those forced into sex, Larsen's decision to make Helga appear happy and content after her experience can only be insulting and offensive. This would be true, however, were we not to take note of Larsen's temporal location of what psychologists term the traumatic experience.[2] As Suzette A. Henke claims, posttraumatic stress disorder occurs "after a crisis precipitated by rape, incest, childhood sexual abuse, unwanted pregnancy, pregnancy-loss, or a severe illness that threatens the integrity of the body and compromises the sense of mastery that aggregates around western notions of harmonious selfhood" (8). But how long after the traumatic experience does it take for the victim to exhibit signs of abuse? While it is clear that Helga's conversion is treated like a rape, her contented response would suggest that the experience is not to be considered traumatic. But if there is a delayed response that could be traced back to the conversion/rape scene, even if it occurs years after the experience, then it could be argued that the conversion is traumatic, despite Helga's initial response.

To illustrate this point, let me argue by comparison. In A. S. Byatt's *Morpho Eugenia*, an aristocrat, Edgar, has been coercing his half sister, Eugenia, into a sexual relationship for a number of years. While Eugenia senses that her brother's actions are inappropriate, she does not quite register the magnitude of the violation. In fact, she likens the experience to masturbation, that is, until the man, Captain Hunt, to whom she is engaged, discovers what Eugenia and Edgar are doing and consequently commits suicide. Only then does Eugenia realize the extent of her brother's transgression, for she says, "that was when I saw—how very terrible—it was—I was" (172). Notice that Eugenia is not traumatized by Captain Hunt's death. Rather, through his suicide she experiences for the first time her sexual relationship with her half brother as traumatic.

For victims of childhood incest, while there may be a sense that the premature sexual act is inappropriate, there is a real danger of naturalizing the experience by making it seem, at least from the closed perspective within which oppressor and oppressed live, that the action is natural. Indeed, when Eugenia tells her husband about her relationship with Edgar, she claims that "he had made me believe it was all perfectly *natural* and so it was *natural*, nothing in us rose up and said—it was—*un*natural" (181). By adopting the mentality that their actions are natural, she minimized the psychological effects that normally ensue from such a sexual violation. But when the action is eventually exposed as a profound violation and a cultural taboo, the victim will register more clearly the magnitude of the transgression, which explains Eugenia's delayed response. It was only when Captain Hunt committed suicide that she was able to identify her brother's incestuous behavior as a serious crime against her person.

Where, then, do we locate the traumatic experience? Does it exist in the moment of violation, even if the individual is not equipped to register that a crime has been committed against his or her person? Or does it exist after the traumatic event occurs, when the person is duly informed of the heinous crime committed? Obviously, there is no need to universalize all traumatic occurrences, for not all experiences result in an identical response within the victim's body. But it can be argued that certain traumatic experiences occur retroactively, that is, when the violated person comes to understand not just that s/he has been abused but also the degree to which s/he has been victimized. Prior to this retrospective awareness, the victim lives in a state of perceived nature by interpreting his or her victimization as normal or, at most, slightly out of the ordinary—"he made me believe it was all perfectly *natural* and so it was *natural*." To my mind, this retrospective traumatic experience best explains the nature of the African American conversion experience, according to the logic of Larsen's novella.

After the violence of the conversion/rape scene, Helga is not only content, she experiences relative happiness for a few years. Because the conversion scene has been pictured in terms of a gang rape, the attentive reader cannot help but wonder how this brutal experience could end in contentment. Granted, the references to rape are not intended to be read literally, but it is hard to imagine that the metaphorical sexual violation is to be dismissed as irrelevant. To understand what makes Helga initially treat the conversion/rape experience positively, we must see how the believers, when converting Helga, strategically structure her inner life such that she interprets experience through the believer's epistemological lens.

Just after Helga accepts the faith, the narrator interjects: "The thing became real" (114). For Helga, the thing that becomes real during her conversion is both God and the absolute truths that the Divine speaks into being. No longer challenging or thinking, she unquestioningly accepts the existence of both (accepting them as an assumption at the level of the subconscious) even though they result in her degradation as well as her people's. Helga's vulnerability to the Reverend Green's manipulation would not be surprising if she had not so emphatically mocked and rejected a preacher in the first chapter. The novella opens with a white preacher telling "Naxos Negroes" that God has called those of African heritage to be "hewers of wood and drawers of water," and to justify this view of the African American subject, he appeals to "Almighty God" as he embellishes "his words with scriptural quotations" (3). Later in the novella, the black preacher uses the same strategy to impose a subservient role on a female subject, but instead of rejecting the preacher and the subservient role he assigns her, Helga succumbs and marries him. After Helga has her conversion, she must learn her role as a God-fearing woman, which means to "be mistress in one's own house, to have a garden, and chickens, and a pig; to have a husband—and to be 'right with God'" (120). When Helga becomes dissatisfied with this role, the Reverend Pleasant Green tells her: "You must . . . trust the Lord more fully" (124). In both instances, religious figures define individuals as a subject, and to justify their representations, they appeal to a divine authority. In other words, African Americans are wood-toting servants, not because the white preacher has cast them into this role but because God has ordained it so. In like manner, women are garden-tending breeders, not because a black preacher has cast them into this role but because God has ordained it so. By telling African Americans and women that these representations of them come not from their personal desire for control but from a neutral and objective source (God), the preachers can effectively mask their personal objectives. Once the God-mentality is established, those who have been invested with spiritual authority can construct individuals within the culture as subordinates. For Larsen, there are two things that make the God-mentality so dangerous: the role the God concept plays in the construction of race and gender subordinates and in the construction and definition of the natural. Understanding these two distinctive features of Larsen's sociocultural critique of faith will explain why Helga so easily exposes the white preacher's sermon as an offensive act of manipulation, but not the Reverend Pleasant Green's.

In the novella, it is important to identify the specific strategies that the religious community uses to enforce belief. First and foremost is the need to stop Helga from thinking, which occurs just after the conversion: "Helga Crane had deliberately stopped thinking" (116). Consequently, the religious Helga does not "reason about anything." Rather, she is simply grateful for feeling "that life was utterly filled with the glory and the marvel of God" (121). Of course, Green would like to keep Helga in this state of nonthinking, so when she begins to question her husband's judgment, he does not reply with an intelligent explanation or encourage her to think seriously. Instead, he deflects Helga's attention from thinking altogether: "If she was inclined to wonder a little just how they were to manage with another child on the way, he would point out to her that her doubt and uncertainty were a stupendous ingratitude. Had not the good God saved her soul from hell-fire and eternal damnation?" (124). Green is making use of the epistemological/ontological recursive loop that I describe in chapter 1. As a spiritual person, Green has epistemological access to spiritual realities. As a black woman, Helga is in the same situation as Fanon's colonized infidels. Green has access to spiritual truth, and as a consequence he can ontologize the world as he deems fit. Because Helga is a culturally designated inferior (as a woman), she cannot question or challenge Green's spiritual system of truth—recall 1 Corinthians in which believers can judge the life of the natural person, whereas the natural person can never judge the life of the believer. It is this closed epistemological/ontological recursive loop that makes Helga incapable of escaping her system of oppression. Indeed, now that the God-thing has become real, Green makes Helga feel ungrateful whenever she has a wayward thought, so she must abandon thinking in order to feel "right with God." To reinforce her emotional leap of faith and to prevent thinking, Green surrounds Helga with models of submission and obedience and then rewards his wife for similar behavior. This is seen most clearly through Helga's interactions with Sary Jones, a sixty-year-old mother of six children. When Helga begins questioning faith, Sary, by dint of her "superhuman" example, chastens and subdues Helga into emotional acceptance of God's mysterious ways: "Before her [Sary] Helga felt humbled and oppressed by the sense of her own unworthiness and lack of sufficient faith" (126). So Helga, once again, stops thinking, and not surprisingly, the community of believers rewards her: "Her husband's flock began to approve and commend this submission and humility to a superior wisdom" (126).

Once thinking ceases, the next strategy is to degrade and empower the convert on two separate levels of existence. The way to do this is to construct a bifurcated subject composed of a spiritual self that exists independently of the material self. During her conversion, Helga notices that the community of believers is composed primarily of women: "Particularly she was interested in the writhings and weepings of the feminine portion, which seemed to predominate" (113). Surrounding Helga, "frenzied women gesticulated, screamed, wept, and tottered" (113). The women's pain and desperation are palpable in this scene, but instead of trying to minimize the grief, the preacher strategically leads the women into prayer by mesmerizing them with his "cadenced chant" until they are in a "savage frenzy" (114). Intensifying misery is crucial, for this is the moment when Helga begins to imagine the existence of an "unknown world" (113), a spiritual reality that transcends the miserable vicissitudes of the physical world. Once Helga begins forging a spiritual self within her body, she will be able to retreat to a place of pure contentment that exists independent of physical suffering. More significantly, however, once this spiritual world is firmly established as an ultimate reality, it is used as the basis for forming judgments about the material world. Consider, for instance, Helga's response to her husband's body odor: "[I]n the certainty of his goodness, his righteousness, his holiness, Helga somehow overcame her first disgust at the odor of sweat and stale garments. She was even able to be unaware of it" (121). So real and superior is Green's spiritual reality that Helga is no longer aware of physical unpleasantries. Significantly, this lack of awareness extends to the political: "The smallest, dirtiest, brown child, barefooted in the fields of muddy roads, was to her an emblem of the wonder of life, of love, and of God's goodness" (121). Instead of taking note of physical hardships and analyzing the reasons why the material conditions of society are as they are, Helga interprets the material world through the lens of divine beneficence. Indeed, spiritual perception has taken so much control of Helga that she is no longer equipped to confront or engage the hardships of the material world: "Her religion was a kind of protective coloring, shielding her from the cruel light of an unbearable reality" (126).

Herein lies the central point about religious belief in *Quicksand*. Because of physical suffering, Helga creates a spiritual reality, a world that transcends human pain and that translates material hardship into an emblem of divine goodness. But for this spiritual epistemology to come into being, human suffering is a prerequisite, a prerequisite that is subsequently negated through spiritual perception. So while material suffering is the basis for the spiritual world's existence, Helga feels that a spiritual interpretation of the material world is legitimate, whereas a material interpretation of the spiritual is not— Paul's natural/spiritual epistemological orientation controls her perceptions at this point. Moreover, while Helga may be degraded on a material level by having been reduced to a domestic drudge, she can lay claim to royalty on a spiritual level now that she is a true child of God. And since only the spiritual world is legitimate, her material degradation is irrelevant.

The next stage of manipulation is to form an inviolable spiritual community. To this end, the community of believers must secure emotional ties that Helga cannot imagine violating. What the religious community does is to posit the existence of a spiritual being that loves Helga unreservedly and unconditionally and whose love is stable and secure. But the way to have emotional access to this divine spiritual being is through the preacher. We get an inkling of the preacher's mediating role just after Helga's conversion. When watching Reverend Green, Helga looks "into his mind," and what she sees is a "mind that was certain that it was secure because it was concerned only with things of the soul, spiritual things" (115). Significantly, in the very next sentence the narrator corrects Helga by indicating that Green's is "actually a mind by habit at home amongst the mere material aspect of things" (115–16). Specifically, what materially motivates Green is sex, the thought of bringing Helga to a state of "ecstacy" and "the pressure of her slim fingers on his heavy arm" (116). But Helga cannot understand Green's physical desires, for in internalizing a spiritual epistemology, she interprets Green's action as symbolic of spiritual harmony, not as a ploy to satisfy sexual desire.

Green's actual motivation is irrelevant, however, for his role is to form a communal bond that bolsters the community's confidence by establishing an alliance with God. Through Green, Helga "had found some One, some Power, who was interested in her" (117). To sustain the illusion in this Power, Green strategically capitalizes on his female congregation's desire to revere and adore him. For instance, when Helga observes a woman openly adoring her husband, she is shocked, that is, until she discovers that "open adoration was the prerogative, the almost religious duty, of the female portion of the flock" (120). This reverential posture has the desired effect of consolidating the community as a chosen people, a sanctified group honored by God. For this reason, Green's "own sense of superiority," instead of offending or repulsing his flock, actually strengthens and bolsters the community, for the greater he is, "the more flattered they were by his notice and small attentions" (120). This sense of Green's superiority, in turn, leads his community to invest his views with authoritative spiritual meaning, which explains why "they hung enraptured on his words" (120). Therefore, for the community to sustain its feeling "that life was utterly filled with the glory and the marvel of God," it benefits tremendously from adoring its preacher, the man who has access to and embodies the spiritual. More importantly, if the community wishes to sustain its feeling of being spiritual royalty in the midst of its material degradation, it must continue to invest the Reverend Green with divine authority; otherwise, its sense of its own spiritual superiority would be exposed as an illusion, a situation that would destroy the founding principle of the community's bond. Not surprisingly, once Helga accepts the emotional logic governing the spiritual community, she establishes an internal censor that prohibits any questioning of the communal bond: "She was at peace, and secure. Surely their two lives were one, and the companionship in the Lord's grace so perfect that to think about it would be tempting providence" (121). The security and peace born of companionship in the Lord's grace is inviolable, so Helga will do nothing to question or challenge the sacred bond.

Once we see how the empowering bond of the community is strategically used to manipulate Helga into belief, we can explain why Green succeeds, where the white preacher fails, in seducing Helga into accepting a degrading role as her natural condition in life. As the burden of Christian living becomes too much for Helga to bear, she wonders: "Or was it only she, a poor weak city-bred thing, who felt that the strain of what the Reverend Mr. Pleasant Green had so often gently and patiently reminded her was a natural thing, an act of God, was almost unbearable?" (125). Notice how Green strategically equates "a natural thing" and "an act of God." His logic could be stated thus: to be natural is to be in touch with God; Green is in touch with God; therefore, he knows what is natural. Obviously, nature for the Reverend is a correct representation of a God-created reality—what Redding refers to as a barely detectable truth that functions "on a level of subconsciousness." Because Helga emotionally accepts the preacher's truth as a God-sanctioned Truth, she ceases to question what is natural, what God has ordained. But even if Helga were to question the legitimacy of Green's claim, her desire to experience peace and security would override her rebellious attitude, because in challenging Green's authority, she would inadvertently deconstruct the spiritual paradise that shields her from her former misery. But once again, after living under the unbearable conditions of Green's truth for a period of time, Helga begins thinking and thereby questions his version of nature: "'But,'" protested Helga, "'I'm always so tired and sick. That can't be natural'" (125). At this point, Helga does not question or challenge God's existence; she interrogates what Green dubs natural. But it will only take a little more thinking for her to question and thereby undermine both.

Indeed, only two chapters later, instead of being governed by her emotions, "Helga had had too much time to think" (133), as the narrator makes clear in the opening sentence of the chapter. It is at this point that Helga, like Eugenia, retroactively experiences her earlier sexual violation as a traumatic experience. What has been happening to Helga is that the material suffering of African Americans and her children has become so overwhelming that she can no longer sustain the belief that physical misery is an emblem of divine goodness. She realizes this just after the birth of her fourth child: "after that long frightfulness, the fourth little dab of amber humanity which Helga had contributed to a despised race was held before her for maternal approval, she failed entirely to respond properly to this sap of consolation for the suffering and horror through which she had passed" (127). Given her earlier experiences with suffering, Helga creates an internal spiritual paradise, a place that not only transcends but also negates the world of human pain. At this point, however, the spiritual interpretation is losing credibility—instead of referring to her child as "an emblem of the wonder of life, of love, and of God's goodness," she refers to the newborn as a "little dab of amber humanity" who belongs "to a despised race."

Helga effectively reverses the spiritual/material interpretation of experience by analyzing the world through the lens of the physical, which ultimately negates the spiritual altogether. Once Helga makes this reversal, she can only look in horror at the effect that belief in God has had on the African American community. Specifically, she exposes religion as a culturally sanctioned method of violating the rights and dignity of African Americans and women: "With the obscuring curtain of religion rent, she was able to look about her and see with shocked eyes this thing she had done to herself. She couldn't, she thought ironically, even blame God for it, now that she knew that He didn't exist" (130). Typical of childhood incest victims, Helga blames herself for succumbing to her own violation, but as I have already shown, the language of her conversion is that of possession and rape, which indicates that she was a victim, not a willing participant. And yet herein lies the dilemma that makes Helga's conversion experience so traumatic long after the initial violation. After berating herself for naïvely believing that God loves all people, Helga turns a critical eye toward the African American community: "What idiotic nonsense she had allowed herself to believe. How could she, how could anyone, have been so deluded? How could ten million black folk credit it when daily before their eyes was enacted its contradiction?" (130). Like Eugenia, Helga retroactively experiences her earlier violation as traumatic, but unlike

Eugenia, what makes Helga's experience so devastating is her realization that her private violation is one among ten million. So the question for Helga is not just how she could have been seduced through belief into such a degrading role but how so many African Americans could have been manipulated as well.

At this point, we are ready to address the most difficult question facing readers of *Quicksand*: why did Larsen use the incredibly offensive metaphor of a gang rape to depict Helga's conversion? The answer to this question lies in the novella's radical critique of ontotheological representation. In the following pages, I want to develop this point by challenging the standard interpretations of *Quicksand*. To date, most scholars ignore the atheism of *Quicksand*, even though the dominant interpretations presuppose an atheistic orientation. As many scholars have already shown, atheism leads to the deconstruction of representation and the death of the subject, and while noted Larsen scholars have been ready and willing to detail Larsen's subversion of representation and deconstruction of subjectivity, they simply refuse to examine how the novella's atheism accounts for these developments. For instance, Barbara Johnson argues that *Quicksand* "provides material for a critique of the conception of the self as a locus of value" (262), but to draw this conclusion, she uses Heinz Kohut's psychological model of child development, which leads her to conclude that Helga's "self-erasure" (258) during her conversion is a consequence of her lack of "early relations with black people" (257). As a black woman in an overtly racist society, Helga "learns to identify with the rejecting other, to desire her own disappearance" (258). Therefore, Helga's self-erasure is inevitable, so it really does not matter that she loses her identity in a religious setting, because Helga was destined, given her upbringing, to erase herself somewhere at some time. But were Johnson to take Larsen's many strategic references to religion into account, she would see that the theological assumptions about the human subject are what account for Helga's self-annihilation. Therefore, that Helga's loss of identity occurs in a church would not be just an incidental locale for what would have inevitably occurred, but rather, her self-annihilation in a church would be the most appropriate venue to dramatize what has been occurring throughout the novella but at a lower frequency.

The failure to detail the significant references to God and religion also plagues Hazel V. Carby's analysis of Larsen's novel. Carby focuses on representation in her interpretation, but instead of attending to the function of the God concept in the construction and reification of representation, she concentrates on the African American dilemma of a split-self. For Carby, Helga's torturous journey through the novella leads "to the burial, not the discovery, of the self" (173). What accounts for this dismal situation is the representational quagmire in which African American women are thrown. As McDowell argues in an analysis that builds on Carby's interpretation, Larsen writes and Helga lives in "the Freudian 1920s, the Jazz Age of sexual abandon and 'free love'" (xii). While the nightlife in a Harlem speakeasy stimulates the young Helga, tempting her to revel in the intensely sensual African American aesthetic form known as jazz, the white community's degrading representations of female black sexuality give Helga pause, leading "to the repression of passion and the repression or denial of female sexuality and desire" (Carby 174). Given Helga's situation, Carby concludes, "Readers are left with the unresolvable" (174) because "the crisis of representation" (169) in an overtly racist society does not provide livable alternatives for the culturally marginalized. What Carby's analysis assumes is that, if societal relations were not racist, then correct representations of human subjectivity would be possible, which would allow a character like Helga to discover her true self. Contra Carby, however, I argue that Larsen's novella does not simply expose and challenge misrepresentations of women and African Americans; it challenges the idea of representation altogether, an interpretation that ultimately leads to the rejection of the belief in a "true self."

According to the logic of this interpretation, rejecting God becomes necessary for Helga, not to create the necessary epistemological conditions for more responsible representations of culturally marginalized figures, but to abolish the naïve assumption that a true representation exists. Let me state my position more clearly by qualifying Cheryl A. Wall's major claim about the novella. According to Wall, Larsen "demonstrates the psychological costs of racism and sexism" (89). For Helga, "she has resisted male definitions of her womanhood." But, "[h]aving no foundation on which to base" a definition of herself as a woman, "Helga never achieves true self-definition" (116). For Wall, the goal—obviously—is "true self-definition," and because Helga lives in a racist and sexist community, she can never find "her true self" (599), as Pamela E. Barnett puts it. But if it can be shown that theological representation is what makes particularly destructive forms of human degradation possible, whether racist or sexist, then we could say that Larsen's novella demonstrates the psychological costs, not of racism and sexism as Wall argues but of the existence of the God concept, because it is belief in God that makes true representation possible. Moreover, it is a *true* representation that makes racism and sexism possible, because without the God concept to legitimize the existence of a true nature, all representations would be exposed as communal constructs, and nothing more. Such an interpretation obviously calls into question Carby's reading. The goal, according to the logic of Larsen's novella, would not be to create more ideal sociopolitical conditions so that individuals could more accurately represent reality and thereby discover their true selves; rather, the goal would be to kill God so that the community could deconstruct representation and abolish the naïve belief in a true self altogether—and such an act would seriously undermine the possibility of the political community to *subject* any group (women or African Americans) into an inferior role. As long as theological representation remains intact, certain groups of people will inevitably be subjected into an inferior state of being, so to create the conditions for a healthier and more just body politic, killing God and the idea of a nature, whether it is a human's nature or a woman's nature, is a psychological and emotional must.

This is the case because belief in God legitimizes the belief in a true representation, what Green refers to as "a natural thing," which is an "act of God." The function of the God concept is to establish a nonideological, nonpolitical, nonconstructed representation of the world and the human, a representation that is accessible to the spiritual person but not to the natural one (1 Corinthians 2). Preachers have privileged epistemological access to God and reality, so their representations of reality are neither politically nor ideologically determined. On the contrary, they are neutral, objective, and true. And yet, to convince individuals that their picture of reality is reality as such, preachers use some of the most ruthless forms of emotional and psychological coercion and manipulation. This explains why Larsen uses a metaphor of rape. The gang rape highlights how believers experience a perverse gratification through their violation of the infidel. As for the unbeliever, once the ontotheological system of representation has been firmly established, individuals can no longer experience agency in their own construction—those who lay claim to spiritual perception can use language to dominate and possess the culturally designated inferior, and the gang rape best articulates what the victim of faith experiences, according to Larsen.

We can now better appreciate Fanon's postcolonial critique of the God concept. Fanon realizes that divine legitimacy is used to insert humans into prefabricated ontological categories: "The serf is in essence different from the knight, but a reference to divine right is necessary to legitimize this statutory difference" (*Wretched* 40). For Larsen, Redding, Fanon, and Wright, it does not really matter if the category is serf or knight, white or black, male or female, for the God concept functions exactly the same in each instance: it legitimizes the existence of a nature that effectively orders social phenomena. But whoever has control of the intellectual means of production can lay epistemological claim to truths about specific human natures, truths that are calculated to benefit those in power by allowing them to ontologize the world and the human, and since believers have constructed an invulnerable epistemological/ontological recursive loop, they can ontologize others so as to serve their own ends. Like Fanon, Larsen recognizes that African Americans and women will never become "human" in the full sense of the word until they take their humanity, something that can occur only when they reject truth, reject nature, but above all, reject God. So I repeat Fanon: "Decolonization is the veritable creation of new men. But this creation owes nothing of its legitimacy to any supernatural power; the 'thing' which has been colonized becomes" human "during the same process by which it frees itself" (*Wretched* 36–37). Tired of being a "thing," Helga rejects the most effective instrument for ontologizing her into a subhuman role; she rejects God.

"Religion is the brainchild of fear, and fear is the parent of cruelty. The greatest evils inflicted on humankind are perpetrated not by pleasure-seekers, self-seeking opportunists, or those who are merely amoral, but by fervent devotees of religion."
Emmanuel Kofi Mensah, "Thoughts from Africa's Leading Secular Humanist Activist"

In "Interrogating Identity," Homi Bhabha claims that "the validity of violence is the very definition of the colonial social space" (43). This claim needs some qualification, however. Given that the world is not a sacred hieroglyph waiting to be correctly named and represented, all discursive systems are a violent imposition upon the world, a conceptual reduction of that which is named to the law of the semiotic sign. In other words, all social space is colonized. However, there is a palpable difference in the intensity of semiotic violence, depending upon the system that is used to colonize space. For Larsen, truthclaims that are ontotheologically constructed presuppose the most violence because God-systems legitimize a spiritual epistemology that allows believers to violently ontologize culturally despised bodies as inferior and thereby gives believers unbridled freedom to subjugate the inferior into a degrading role that is dubbed natural. To minimize epistemic violence, to make it more democratic and productive, Larsen suggests that the culture must secularize social space by constructing it as provisional and fluid, alternately pluralistic and amorphous.

That an oppressive ontotheological system has been an omnipresent force dominating the African American community is clear from Larsen's strategic references to religion throughout the novella. For instance, because of her job, Helga must go, "unwillingly, to a meeting, held in a large church—as were most of Harlem's uplift activities" (49). So present is religion that even in the jazz club, where religion appears to be absent, the panoptic religious eye casts its critical glance on Helga as she enters the speakeasy:[3] "Entering the waiting doorway, they descended through a furtive, narrow passage, into a vast subterranean room. Helga smiled, thinking this was one of those places characterized by the righteous as hell" (58).[3] When Helga goes to Denmark, it would seem that she has finally escaped religion, for there are no references to it during her stay. But as soon as she returns to Harlem, "It was as if she passed from the heavy solemnity of a church service to a gorgeous care-free revel" (96).

While religion may be spatially present throughout the novella, Helga discovers that it has been eternally there as a force to control and entrap her. For instance, when Helga is at a breaking point, she hears a religious song "which she was conscious of having heard years ago—hundreds of years it seemed" (110–11). A little later, after her conversion, Helga sinks "back into the mysterious grandeur and holiness of far-off simpler centuries" (114). By turning her life over to God, she enters into a centuries-old tradition of sublime and holy belief, but after exposing faith as a conceptual system used to enslave and degrade African Americans and women, she considers religion an age-old disaster: "She knew only that, in the hideous agony that for interminable hours—no, centuries—she had borne, the luster of religion had vanished" (129). And the more she reflects on the devastating consequences of belief, the more she realizes how weak and vulnerable she has become: "It seemed hundreds of years since she had been strong" (134). The references to centuries are always connected with a religious mentality, so any attempt to break with the religious mind-set means more than just rejecting a current system of belief—it means rejecting centuries of an established tradition.

Significantly, in the closing chapters when Helga finally confesses herself an atheist ("she knew now. He [God] wasn't there. Didn't exist" [130]), she makes her most significant discoveries about the African American community's acceptance of faith: "Into the yawning gap of unspeakable brutality had gone, too, her belief in the miracle and wonder of life. Only scorn, resentment, and hate remained—and ridicule. Life wasn't a miracle, a wonder. It was, for Negroes at least, only a great disappointment" (130). While Helga may be extremely critical of herself and others for crediting belief, Larsen has carefully and strategically documented why not believing is nearly impossible: the structures of belief have been so deeply embedded within the society that cultural space and time have been religiously encoded. For this reason, it is not surprising that Helga and many other African Americans and women succumb to the faith that ultimately functions to subject them into an inferior social role.

Given this atheistic interpretation of the novel, we can now explain why Helga's rejection of religion is so merciless and unforgiving. Psychologically and emotionally, African Americans and women are strategically violated and degraded by making them yearn for a saving truth, a truth that—ironically—ontologizes individuals as things, something subhuman. Moreover, since both groups are deprived of a first-rate education, they do not develop the thinking skills necessary for exposing the ontotheological system of representation as the most effective method for subjecting the culturally marginalized into an inferior being. So African Americans and women, because of the abuse they suffer, turn to religion for solace, but their imagined need for religion is precisely what prevents them from escaping their situation as culturally created inferiors. Indeed, religion is the most effective instrument for making individuals content with their role as cultural inferiors. The narrator subtly underscores this ambivalent situation when Helga has her conversion by saying that "in that moment she [Helga] was lost—or saved" (113). By turning to God, Helga is saved from an emotional breakdown. Since the culture does not create spaces where people like Helga can find meaning, fulfillment, and purpose, she makes a leap of faith, which gives her hope for "a chance at stability, at permanent happiness" (117). However, through her conversion, she loses her dignity and self-respect as a woman and an African American. Through faith she has been trained to think of herself as a garden-tending breeder who lives in "submission and humility to a superior wisdom" (126), that is, to her husband the preacher. But after Helga realizes how the leap of faith has both saved and further damaged her, she clearly articulates the ambivalent but ultimately destructive consequences of faith: "Her mind, swaying back to the protection that religion had afforded her, almost she wished that it had not failed her. An illusion. Yes. But better, far better, than this terrible reality. Religion had, after all, its uses. It blunted the perceptions. Robbed life of its crudest truths. Especially it had its uses for the poor—and the blacks" (133). Religion is an illusion, one that blunts the perceptions, but it does provide an emotional and psychological sanctuary for the walking wounded.

But is the feeling of security that religion provides enough to compensate for the abuse that individuals suffer by being traumatized into a community of faith? Granted, believers do not have the epistemological capacity to recognize the degree to which they have been abused (recall the narrator's comment that religion "blunted the perceptions") because they have resigned themselves to their God-prescribed roles. But just because they cannot identify their victimization as victimization, does that mean that they have not been victimized? Had Eugenia's fiancée not committed suicide, she may might never have realized that she had been horribly violated ("that was when I saw—how very terrible—it was—I was."). For Helga, it is not until she denies God's existence that she sees how the community of believers has violated her ("With the obscuring curtain of religion rent, she was able to look about her and see with shocked eyes this thing that she had done to herself"). But had she not developed the thinking skills that enabled her to see behind the obscuring curtains of religion, she may might never have been able to see. And since not seeing means that those "ten million black folk" will continue to accept their divinely prescribed role as cultural inferiors, they will be just a thing, as Fanon claims. The only way to effect liberation for African Americans and women would be widespread atheism.

To highlight specifically the necessity of atheism, Larsen invites her reader to see the connection between the religious mind-set and a destructive institution of higher education. Just after her experience with the white preacher in the first chapter, Helga reflects on the nature of pedagogy at a school like Naxos: "This great community, she thought, was no longer a school. It had grown into a machine. It was now a show place in the black belt, exemplification of the white man's magnanimity, refutation of the black man's inefficiency. Life had died out of it. It was, Helga decided, now only a big knife with cruelly sharp edges ruthlessly cutting all to a pattern, the white man's pattern. Teachers as well as students were subjected to the paring process, for it tolerated no innovations, no individualisms" (4). In a world in which ontotheology dominates, there is a nature to being (ontology), and humans have epistemological access to it. But if belief in reality requires an epistemological act that is identical to the traditional leap of faith (a theological epistemology that presupposes the belief in a conceptual reality that is unseen, hence the suggestion that ontology is theological), then ontology would be as much a construction of the imagination as the God concept. From an atheist perspective, therefore, since there is no conceptual reality out there waiting to be discovered (no mind-independent truth, as I have discussed in chapter

2), education should not function to disclose reality. On the contrary, when individuals claim to know reality, they are not naturally and objectively representing a mind-independent truth; they are creating a truth that they wish others to accept as real. Notice how Larsen's narrator uses the image of a knife to depict the violent function of education at Naxos. Epistemologically, the pattern preexists language and the human according to an ontotheological system of knowledge, which means that "Naxos Negroes," if they are to be right with God, must discover what that pattern is and then force their persons to conform to that pattern. And since the preacher has access to this pattern, he discovers/creates the most suitable one for "Naxos Negroes," and they must ruthlessly cut their bodies down to it.

Larsen uses this knife image for the same reason she uses the rape metaphor—to underscore the violence at the core of a seemingly natural act. On the surface, converting a person to belief in God seems harmless, but after exposing how the conversion is strategically used to *subject* individuals to a degrading social role, the conversion can be seen as a traumatic violation of a person's dignity. In like manner, on the surface, education seems harmless, but once it is exposed as a "method" for creating individuals as "things," it can then be seen as a profound instance of politically and culturally sanctioned abuse. To appreciate the nature of this violence, one must first understand the atheist's principle of designification. Objects exist in the world, but there is no ideal language for signifying those objects. Therefore, when "humans" name the world or the human, they perform an act of epistemic violence, though this violence does not need to be overt to be violent. In fact, the most effective violence occurs through the seemingly natural acts of conversion and education. Because these acts are so subtle, because they seem totally natural, because they are perpetrated, as Emmanuel Kofi Mensah claims, by selfless people with seemingly good intentions, they are almost impossible to identify as dangerous and destructive. But once they are exposed as strategic methods for *subjecting* individuals into cultural inferiors, the culturally marginalized feel totally violated.

This explains why Larsen places the education scene immediately after the white preacher scene. The assumptions implied in ontotheological conversion and education are quite similar; moreover, both have devastating consequences, especially for culturally marginalized figures, because they disable marginalized people on both a political and personal level. Instead of dynamically creating themselves with each passing generation, Naxos students allow those in power to produce them by *subjecting* them as it were to a cultural role that benefits those in power. It is for this reason that Helga vehemently rejects Naxos education: "it wasn't the fault of those minds back of the diverse colored faces. It was, rather, the fault of the method, the general idea behind the system" (4). The general idea behind this system is that truth preexists language, that the preachers have access to it, and that individuals must force their bodies to conform to those truths. What would be a more effective pedagogical approach, given the logic of *Quicksand*? A naïve answer would be a system of education that would allow African Americans to represent African Americans as they really are. To expose the dangers of this new approach to representation, Larsen creates Reverend Pleasant Green. While Green may be in a position to better represent the black community, he uses the same ontotheological methods to *subject* women into an inferior role as the white preacher uses to *subject* African Americans. In other words, both men develop a relationship to knowledge that legitimizes their positions of power while simultaneously disempowering others. The only difference for Green is that a different group is in power and another group (women) is now *subjected* into an inferior role.

To empower Naxos students, the novella suggests, the whole method of ontotheological education must be deconstructed. This means that on a personal level, instead of presupposing that a truth-representation preexists language and that individuals must conform their bodies to this representation, post-ontotheological education demands that students explore who created and controls truth-representations. After students understand that representation is the most effective method for producing individuals as subjects, they can then begin the process of taking control of their own psychogenesis by controlling their own representation. To put this in Fanon's language, the colonized "thing" can only become "human" when it identifies the subtle colonizing tactics of ontotheological representation and then claims its own identity through a process of self-creation and self-definition. According to this interpretation, atheism is politically necessary in order for African Americans and women to experience individual and communal empowerment, that is, the freedom to construct and define themselves, rather than being constructed by the dominant culture.

The danger, at this point, is to think that a more democratic approach to ontotheological representation would solve the problem for the culturally marginalized. Such an approach, however, would preserve the idea of a true subject (a true self), which would obviously make possible the danger of one group claiming to be better stationed to represent another group's essential nature. Larsen illustrates this danger most clearly through the character of Axel Olsen, the artist Helga nearly marries when living in Denmark. When he shows Helga a painting that he has done of her, Helga is disgusted, but Olsen assures her: "I think that my picture of you is, after all, the true Helga Crane" (88). For Helga, however, the picture "wasn't, she contended, herself at all, but some disgusting sensual creature with her features" (89). By hanging on to a notion of a true self, an assumption at the heart of ontotheological representation, there will always be the danger of being *subjected* into an essentially inferior role—the white preacher is better situated to know what those of African heritage really are, while the black preacher is better situated to know what women really are. By killing God and deconstructing representation, Naxos students must take an active role in creating themselves rather than learning to know themselves. According to this view of education, the God concept is not just irrelevant; it is absolutely detrimental.

"If the concept of God has any validity or any use, it can only be to make us larger, freer, and more loving. If God cannot do this, then it is time we got rid of Him."
James Baldwin, *The Fire Next Time*

Larsen's decision to use the metaphor of a gang rape is, given the logic of this book, the most appropriate image to signify the function of belief within culture. For Larsen and many African American atheists, the problem with the God-thing and the nature-concept is that they are so effective, which explains Helga's comment about the ten million black folk being seduced into belief. The strength of Larsen's novella as an instance of the sociocultural critique of faith is Helga's extremely strong and independent character. If Helga could be manipulated into belief, even if it is only for a few years, then the community of believers must have at its disposal extraordinary methods of manipulation and control. The nature concept is that controlling mechanism. Once the God-mentality is linked to the nature concept, the community of believers has the freedom to subject a person into an extremely degrading role, and the victim will not even recognize that he or she has been victimized. To highlight how this system of victimization functions, Larsen makes use of a theory of delayed trauma. Only after Helga becomes an atheist can she finally understand that she is a rape victim of the religious community. Conversely, had she not become an atheist, she would never have discovered that she has had been victimized—her condition as a domestic drudge would be "a natural thing, an act of God," just as her conversion experience, instead of being a gang rape, would be the work of a loving Deity.

Now we can understand why God is so ugly, according to African American atheists. The God concept has been the most effective instrument for those in control of the intellectual means of "subject" production to ontologize culturally designated inferiors as inferior. Because God is an unassailable concept, most people could never imagine that it has been used to perpetuate the wicked idea of human inferiority. But for those who do, like Helga, there is a feeling that they have been traumatically violated, gang raped in a sense by the lordly rulers of signifying systems. It is only after they identify the God-created truth in their bodies as truth-illusions that they can recognize how they have been victimized at the level of the subconscious. Larsen's delayed trauma metaphor highlights not only the destructively violent sadism at the core of the religious production of meaning, but also the super-subtle nature of this experience, which can only be detected through an understanding of the way that signifying systems violently ontologize the world and humans. Not surprisingly, it is only former-believers-become-atheists, like Helga, who have been able to expose the ruthless sadism associated with belief in God.

4

Langston Hughes
The Sociopolitical Structuring of God, Desire, and the Law

"God probably thought that everything was lovely in the world."
Langston Hughes, "Trouble with the Angels"

Like Wright and Larsen, Langston Hughes is a severe critic of the God concept, but unlike Wright and Larsen, he focuses his attention almost exclusively on sociopolitical and sociocultural systems instead of tortured inner lives. Therefore, if we approach Hughes's fiction with an eye for the psychological trauma of people who have suffered because of oppressive theistic systems (like Cross Damon or Helga Crane), we will find, for the most part, the fiction wanting. But if we see the writings as an attempt to expose the way the God concept functions to justify an oppressive sociopolitical system, then the fiction will be as illuminating as it is poignant.

Hughes's ultimate conclusions, which are certainly not calculated to delight many, are shocking. In the tradition of one of his most powerful literary forebears, Walt Whitman, Hughes desires to pass on to his reader "the password primeval," which is "the sign of democracy" (Whitman 43).[1] But what makes Hughes's view so stunning is not his claim that America is not really a democracy, nor that the American political system bears a striking resemblance to Hitler's Germany, but that democracy can only be realized within an atheistic context.

"Nobody could see God. He was safely housed in the quiet home of
a conservative Negro professor, guarded by two detectives."
Langston Hughes, "Trouble with the Angels"

Let me begin this chapter by identifying how the God concept functions, according to Hughes. In the tradition of Feuerbach, Larsen, Redding, Fanon, and Wright, Hughes treats the God-concept not as a mind-independent reality but as a psychological projection, the mental product of what people desire. The 1924 poem "Gods" articulates this view succinctly. The poem begins with a reference to "The ivory gods, / And the ebony gods," which "Sit silently on their temple shelves." The suggestion here, of course, is that the black and white gods are either impotent or inactive. But what makes the poem so blasphemous is Hughes's concluding observation that the gods are nothing more than human constructions:

Yet the ivory gods,
And the ebony gods,
And the gods of diamond-jade
Are only silly puppet gods
That the people themselves
Have made. (37)

The references to all gods, whether black or white, as puppets are crucial to Hughes's scathing critique of religion. An audience sees the puppet, but not the person pulling the strings, the individual who gives life to the lifeless object. The concealment of the puppeteer ensures a certain freedom, for if the puppet says something offensive or degrading, the puppeteer can claim that it is the puppet's character, not the puppeteer, who is at fault. In essence, the puppet is the perfect frontperson, the one who represents the views of the person pulling the strings but also the one who must assume responsibility for any unpleasant consequences.

For Hughes, calling the gods puppets is a calculated effort to expose the concept of God as a semiotic vacuity, an empty signifier that humans manipulate and control in order to further their sociopolitical agenda with impunity. The God concept, whatever its forms, takes its cue from the human puppeteer. Therefore, the question for Hughes is never what God is; that is an absurd and incoherent question. Rather, it is what the human puppeteer decides God should be. According to this view, whoever has the political and cultural power to pull God's strings, in other words, the power to control the intellectual means of production, can use the God concept for whatever purpose he or she deems fit.

The work in which Hughes examines this idea of God as puppet most thoroughly and extensively is his 1935 short story "Trouble With the Angels." On the surface, this story dramatizes the struggles of black thespians who travel across America performing a play about the experiences of black folk in heaven. An uplifting play, it is calculated to improve race relations, for the white audiences that see it are given a wholesome perspective of black life. The problem is that, given the tremendous success of the play, African Americans, specifically in Washington, D.C., desire to see the performance as well, but since black people are not allowed in white theaters in the nation's capital during the time of the story, only white people can attend a performance. In protest, one performer, Johnny Logan, urges his fellow actors to stage a strike, but in the final moments of the story, Logan is arrested and the play goes on. A simple story of race prejudice in the United States, the tale's ending underscores the helpless and dire political conditions for black Americans.

The story, however, becomes much more complicated if we take into account the names of the characters. The main character in the play is named God, and Johnny Logan is "a black angel." Cleverly, the narrator never mentions the real name of the actor portraying God, which gives Hughes (and me, as should be clear from my epigraphs in this chapter) some freedom to play with the God concept. For instance, instead of saying Tom "probably thought that everything was lovely in the world," a view that many people hold, Hughes's narrator says: "God probably thought that everything was lovely in the world." This claim is both comic and tragic. God is supposed to know everything, and since the living conditions for black people in America were anything but "lovely" at this time, we can only smirk at God's innocence and ignorance. On the tragic side, since God is just a silly puppet that people in power have created, God's stupid remark fails to acknowledge the horrible plight of African Americans. And if God cannot recognize or understand the suffering of black people in America, there is virtually no hope of righting the culture's political wrongs.

As a puppet, God is at the beck and call of those who have economic and political power. That Hughes would have his reader see God as a political puppet is obvious by his decision to set the story in "Washington, the capital of the United States" (124). God "thought it would be fine for the good white people of the Capital to see him—a colored God—even if Negroes couldn't" (120). But as the narrator makes clear, while ordinary black folk are regularly discriminated against, specifically denied acceptable living quarters, God gets special treatment nonetheless: "Only the actor who played God would sometimes, by the hardest, achieve accommodations in a white hotel, or be put up by some nice white family, or be invited to the home of the best Negroes in town. Thus God probably thought that everything was lovely in the world" (120). Why does the black God get preferential treatment? Hughes supplies an answer in two other short stories and one poem.

In the powerful closing story of *The Ways of White Folks*, "Father and Son," Bert, the illegitimate son of Georgia plantation owner Colonel Norwood, returns home from college. Resolved not "to be a *white folks' nigger*" (228), Bert demands that his father acknowledge him as his son and treat him with dignity. Incensed, Colonel Norwood orders his son "to work in the fields" (229), but Bert, who is just as stubborn as his father, defies the order. Since the black population is already overwrought because of the unjust Scottsboro trials, Colonel Norwood orders "the colored rural Baptist minister to start a revival and keep it going until he said stop" (230).[2] In this story, the Baptist minister is the white man's most effective instrument for pacifying potentially rebellious and unruly black folk. Indeed, the narrator specifies how white folk have made use of Christianity and its ministers to their own advantage: "White folks had always found revivals a useful outlet for sullen overworked darkies. As long as they were singing and praying, they forgot about the troubles of this world. In a frenzy of rhythm and religion, they laid their cross at the feet of Jesus" (230). Jesus suffered and died on the Cross. Oppressed African Americans have been suffering a similar fate ("Nigger Christ / On the cross / Of the South" [Hughes, "Christ" 143]), but like Christ, they can look forward to the heavenly bliss of the afterlife, the reward of the righteous. Such is the line that white plantation owners like Colonel Norwood want black ministers to preach to the faithful. Therefore, if white people can control black ministers, specifically their interpretation of Christianity, they can control God.

Let us look more closely at a passage that specifically underscores the economic value of the God concept for someone like Colonel Norwood: "Poor over-worked Jesus! Somehow since the War, he hadn't borne that cross so well. Too heavy, it's too heavy! Lately, Negroes seem to sense that it's not Jesus' cross, anyhow, it's their own. Only old people praise King Jesus any more. On the Norwood plantation, Bert's done told the young people to stop being white folks' niggers. More and more, the Colonel felt it was Bert who brought trouble into the Georgia summer. The revival was a failure" (230). Black people are starting to realize that the Jesus idea has been constructed in such a way that it justifies their subordinate position within the culture. In essence, African Americans are starting to understand that Jesus is a puppet and that the white man is the puppeteer. Let me be more specific. Jesus as innocent lamb sacrificed and slain on the altar of political injustice is the perfect God concept, for in glorifying Christ's suffering on the cross, white people can convince black people that, through their suffering, they have become one with Jesus. And through this psychological identification with Christ, African Americans can

treat their worldly suffering as naught in light of their heavenly reward. But
if the Jesus concept is the white community's construction that is used to
vindicate an oppressive politics, then the black person's earthly cross would
not be just a moment of suffering as a gateway to eternal bliss. It would be
their only reality. This is what the black folk in Hughes's story, like Helga in
Quicksand, are starting to realize. What African Americans are experiencing
is not "Jesus' cross, . . . it's their own."

This idea of the suffering Christ on the cross, who empowers those who
have suffered in his name, has not served the black community well. But it
has served the white community well. By understanding that whites are the
puppeteers pulling the Jesus-puppet strings, blacks have come to the devastating conclusion that their suffering is theirs and theirs alone. Of course,
"old people" still "praise King Jesus," but the young blacks, college-educated
people like Bert, have been able to expose Christ as a puppet.[3] Notice, for instance, how the narrator's logic captures the essence of Hughes's view of God
as puppet. Just after the narrator mentions that only old people still praise
Christ, the passage shifts to Bert, who tells the "young people to stop being
white folks' niggers." By continuing to praise Christ, Hughes implies, the
old folk remain "white folks' niggers." Therefore, to stop being "white folks'
niggers," the young people must stop glorifying Christ. And they do this, for
as the paragraph concludes, "The revival was a failure." Given the failure of
the revival, black people will be less inclined to labor for virtually nothing.
In short, without a Christian-based theology that glorifies suffering, Colonel
Norwood is facing financial ruin, for without a Jesus-puppet who will bear
the black folks' cross, African Americans no longer have an incentive for accepting degrading living conditions.

Hughes examines the socioeconomic value of the God concept for the
white community again in his 1935 short story "Professor," which was first
published under the title "Dr. Brown's Decision." African American professor T. Walton Brown has achieved considerable notoriety for his book *The
Sociology of Prejudice*. Given his success, he has been invited to dine with Mr.
Ralph P. Chandler, a white American philanthropist who makes substantial
contributions to "Negro education" (102). Also present at the dinner is "Dr.
Bulwick of the local municipal college—a college that Dr. Brown recalled
did *not* admit Negroes" (104). During a conversation, Dr. Bulwick tells Dr.
Brown, "The American Negro must not be taken in by Communism" (105).
Dr. Brown agrees, as he must, since his potential patron, Mr. Chandler, is
a robust capitalist. Not surprisingly, after everyone agrees that communism

would be ruinous for African Americans, the story shifts to the value of Christianity: "'In your *Sociology of Prejudice*,' said Dr. Bulwick, 'I highly approve of the closing note, your magnificent appeal to the old standards of Christian morality and the simple concepts of justice by which America functions'" (106). What makes this story so interesting (and significantly different from "Father and Son") is the way it depicts a black leader who is rewarded for disseminating Christianity to African Americans. In "Father and Son," the black Baptist minister is clearly used to pacify rebellious African Americans, but we are never given a glimpse of the cozy relationship between Colonel Norwood and the black minister. In "Professor," we see specifically how a black leader will be rewarded for using Christianity to keep black folk in their place.

For instance, just after Dr. Bulwick applauds the Christian conclusion of *Sociology of Prejudice*, much is disclosed about Dr. Brown's motivation for concluding the book as he did: "'Yes,' said Dr. Brown, nodding his dark head and thinking suddenly how on six thousand dollars a year he might take his family to South America in the summer where for three months they wouldn't feel like Negroes. 'Yes, Dr. Bulwick,' he nodded, 'I firmly believe as you do that if the best elements of both races came together in Christian fellowship, we would solve this problem of ours'" (106). With a substantial contribution from a philanthropist like Mr. Chandler, Dr. Brown will achieve much for his people; he will be able to take his family abroad. But to get Mr. Chandler's support, the Professor must give white folk exactly what they want. In this case, as it was in "Father and Son," it is a Christian theology that can be used to indoctrinate black folk. To be expected, the "sane and conservative way in which Dr. Brown presented his case delighted the philanthropic heart of the Chandlers" (106). And Dr. Brown knows that the "white people were delighted" with him: "He could see it in their faces, just as in the past he could always tell as a waiter when he had pleased a table full of whites by tender steaks and good service" (107). Hughes's irony is unmistakable at this point. Dr. Brown may be a highly regarded professor, but he has not climbed very high on the ladder of human dignity, for he still is in the position of a server, someone who can say and think only what his white patron/master will allow him to say and think. And what he says and thinks about God is exactly what white leaders want him to say and think.

If there were any uncertainty about Hughes's irony in this story, the concluding sentence should dispel all doubt: "As the car sped him back toward town, Dr. Brown sat under its soft fur rug among the deep cushions and thought how with six thousand dollars a year earned by dancing properly to the tune of Jim Crow education, he could carry his whole family to South America for a summer where they wouldn't need to feel like Negroes" (107). Dr. Brown is exactly what the white patron needs and wants, someone who will persuade his own people to dance "properly to the tune of Jim Crow education," which will be accomplished through Christian teachings that will "solve this problem of ours." For being attentive to the white community's desires and producing a work that would pacify his people, the Professor will be richly compensated.

The function of the Jesus-puppet to justify white superiority and black subordination, as seen in "Father and Son" and "Professor," explains Hughes's vitriolic poem "Goodbye Christ." In this poem, the narrator claims that Christ and the Bible are dead now because "The popes and the preachers've / Made too much money from it" through their enslavement of many people. So that such slavery can never be perpetrated again, the narrator tells Christ to "Beat it on away from here now," for as the narrator concludes: "And no-body's gonna sell ME / To a king, or a general, / Or a millionaire" (166–67). Important to note is that Hughes does not oppose Christ because Jesus is essentially a bad man or an evil god. He rejects Christ and all God concepts because they are empty signifiers (puppets), semiotic vacuities that those in power can so easily manipulate and control in order to justify and perpetuate whatever political agenda they desire.

"God received the delegation in his dressing room and wept about his inability to do anything concerning the situation."

Langston Hughes, "Trouble with the Angels"

Given this consistent treatment of the God concept as a puppet at the beck and call of those with economic and political power, we are in a better position to understand the significance of God's preferential treatment from the white community during His stay in the nation's capital in "Trouble With the Angels." White people must treat the black God well, for it is through the God concept that they will best be able to control African Americans. Let me briefly outline how whites politically control the black God throughout the story.

In this story, the central political issue is the black person's legal right to view a performance of African Americans in heaven. To obtain this right, "Washington Negroes" and several African American organizations beseech God to intervene on their behalf. But such a petition puzzles God, since "for many years white folks had not allowed Negroes in Washington to see any shows—not even in the churches, let alone in theaters!" (121). Why blacks should suddenly decide that they should be admitted confuses God, so He refuses to answer their petition. But then, in the next paragraph, the reader is given more insight into God's decision not to assist disenfranchised African Americans. He is being paid well and he is well known, a situation that clearly brings Dr. Brown of "Professor" to mind. What God is in and of Himself is an absurd question in Hughes's world. God is only what people in power allow Him to be. In a nation under God, in which the secular laws reflect the will of the Divine, God (and therefore the laws) will be (as a representation) what those in power want Him (them) to be. Whoever controls the God concept can determine the law. In the context of "Trouble With the Angels," God endorses a view that would have African Americans dance properly to the tune of Jim Crow. And so long as God (via his ministers like Dr. Brown and the black Baptist minister) fulfills His duty, He will be richly rewarded.

At issue here is law and the Law, specifically insofar as the God concept plays an instrumental role in their construction. The Law is coeternal with the Divine, a metaphysical reality that does not just provide mortal beings with a code of conduct for suitable behavior on this terrestrial ball. It is the precondition for the very existence of individual laws and being itself, the necessary condition under which being could come to be. That we should think of our earthly being in relation to laws in a legal sense and laws in the sense of a condition of being (for instance, the laws of our nature) is the logical product of a primordial Law, the first Law, the uncreated Law that is inseparable from Divine Being and the Being of the Divine. From Sophocles' *Antigone* and Plato's dialogues, through Augustine's *City of God* and Dante's *Divine Comedy*, to the United States' Declaration of Independence, the secular laws have been determined in western culture by the Divine Law, so if we, as a culture, would wish to know the inalienable rights of humans and the inviolable laws of the universe, we must first acknowledge the existence of the primordial Law, the Law that is coeternal with the Divine. According to this theological system, Truths, as disclosed through Divine Revelation or discerned through a spiritual epistemology, cannot be debased by referring to them as mere human inventions; as God-created realities, they would exist even if there were no humans. Therefore, those who have access to these Laws should be in the position to institute a just political system.

Within the context of this Divine/human view of the Law/law, the God concept has three separate functions. First, from a philosophical perspective, the Law, which is the foundation of an epistemologically accessible system of justice, is infallible, so when God decides that black folk should not attend a performance of a play by black actors, there is a corresponding sense of logical necessity and inevitability. After all, "God was right" (124), and if humans want to do the right and just thing, then they must heed the secular law, which is based on the Divine Law. To question the Law, therefore, is to question God, to thwart the divinely established conditions for securing justice.

From a psychological perspective, the God concept functions to persuade culturally disenfranchised people to internalize a system that alienates themselves them from their own needs and desires. To be fully human, to be psychologically and culturally empowered as full-fledged humans, black folk must be accorded the legal right to participate, at all levels, in the culture. They must be given equal access to all that the culture affords. And the secular laws must ensure the right of all people to participate in its social institutions. But when black folk acknowledge that "God was right" to bar them from seeing a black performance, they are implicitly accepting their inferiority. Imagine how we would interpret the story had the black thespians said, "They pretended that God was right." Here's how our interpretation would run: on the surface, the black players know that God's decision is unjust, but they accept it nevertheless, primarily because it is their only option. But beneath the surface, they know that God is a puppet who is controlled by white folk, so God is not really right. They are just pretending that he is right for reasons of political expediency. But what the black players actually say is that "God was right." Because this passage is so crucial, let me quote it in context: "It was all right to talk about being a man and standing up for your race, and all that—but hell, even an actor has to eat. Besides, God was right. It was a great play, a famous play! They ought to hold up its reputation. It did white folks good to see Negroes in such a play. Logan must be crazy!" (124). Logan is a man who refuses to be treated as an inferior: "He believed in fighting prejudice, in bucking against the traces of discrimination and Jim Crow, and in trying to knock down any white man who insulted him" (122). And while nearly all the black players initially agree with Logan to stage a strike, God persuades them to abandon this view. Notice the progression of logic in the passage. At first, the thespians tentatively affirm a person's right to stand up for his or her race. But then practical considerations, like eating, assume priority. To vindicate their position, the players observe that God is right, which leads them to justify the right of only white people to see the play and their decision to demonize Logan.

In terms of the black thespians' sense of their psychological selves, accepting God's word means internalizing their own inferiority; it implicitly means rejecting the view that they are the ontological equals of whites. Now, of course, one could argue that the thespians have virtually no option, that they have been forced into their unfortunate position, so they do the practical thing by capitulating, which would suggest that they have not necessarily internalized their own inferiority. Were that the case, however, the thespians would recognize that Logan's view is right, but not politically expedient. But what the thespians say is that God is right and that Logan is crazy, which is to say that blacks should dance to the tune of Jim Crow and that Logan is crazy to insist on being treated as an equal. In essence, the God concept effectively persuades the thespians to negate their desire for equal treatment before the law. But more than that, at the level of desire, it makes them comfortably accept their own degradation. Notice the diction when the players finally conclude that God is right: "It was a great play, a famous play! They ought to hold up its reputation. It did white folks good to see Negroes in such a play." Here there is no tone of indignation over the indignity they must suffer; there is a willful acceptance of the situation as a necessary posture before the law. And significantly, it is the God concept that has psychologically convinced them that they should willingly accept this inferior condition.

"God arrived with motorcycle cops in front of his car."

Langston Hughes, "Trouble with the Angels"

Once the God concept legitimizes the law and then convinces whites and blacks that the law is righteous and just, then the culture's enforcers would have the legal authority to identify, criminalize, and ultimately punish dissenters. In short, the third function of the God concept is to authorize a legal apparatus that can be deployed to punish with impunity those who refuse to submit to the normativized edicts of those in power. Within the context of "Trouble With the Angels," God is the figure that authorizes detectives to cart Logan "off to jail—for disturbing the peace" (125). But it is important to keep in mind what a justification of a legal apparatus entails. As legal scholar Robert Cover has so brilliantly and insightfully argued in "Violence and the Word," the construction of the law requires a communal emotional assent, a feeling that the law is exactly as it should be.[4] Indeed, even those who are the victims of the law assent to its righteousness and inevitability. This is the case because there is an originary violence that structures political subjects at the level of desire such that their interpretation of the world corresponds to the law. In the essay, "The Force of Law," Jacques Derrida insightfully describes this originary violence within the context of a legal system: "there is the distinction between two kinds of violence in law, in relation to law (*droit*): the founding violence, the one that institutes and positions law . . . and the violence that conserves, the one that maintains, confirms, insures the permanence and enforceability of law" (31). Constructing subjects such that they willingly accept sociopolitical conditions as legitimate and even necessary originates in a moment of psychological violence, an assault, reminiscent of Helga Crane's experience during the conversion scene in *Quicksand*, that orients individuals at the level of desire in relation to the law, whether the law benefits them or not. According to this view, the law is not a public edict that violently compels individuals to submit to it against their will; it is an internalized desire, violently projected into individuals, such that they willingly interpret and experience the world and self through the law. Indeed, even when the law functions to demoralize and dehumanize a person, there is an emotional sense that it is exactly what it should be. Hughes would agree with Derrida's idea of the founding violence of the law, but he would add that it is the God concept that plays a crucial role in the formation of the law-abiding citizens' desire, desire that is instituted and constituted in relation to a belief in the existence of a metaphysical, mind-independent Law.

Take, for instance, the thespians' decision to strike in order to force the theater establishment to allow blacks to attend the play. Initially, the players are enraged: "black angels—from tenors to basses, sopranos to blues singers—were up in arms. Everybody in the cast, except God, agreed to strike" (123). Outrage, indignation, fury—these are the emotions that best describe the thespians' first response to the discrimination against African Americans. But once God declares the discrimination "right," and once the black community accepts God's decree, the players have a completely opposite emotional response: "Nobody really wanted to strike" (125). No longer a desire to oppose the "white stage manager" and "the New York producing officer" (124) in order to secure "race pride, decency, or elementary human rights" (125), no longer a desire to use a strike to combat an unjust law, but a desire not to strike dominates. At this point, the unjust law is not in conflict with the thespians' desire; their desire is perfectly in sync with the law, and it is God (and the coeternal Divine Law) that has made such a state of affairs possible. In short, the God concept functions not so much to ground an unjust law as it does to structure desire such that it coincides with dehumanizing and demoralizing laws.

If the God concept functions to structure desire in relation to the law, then whoever controls the God-puppet will be in the position to construct law-abiding citizens at the level of desire. Such is the central idea of "Trouble With the Angels," and Hughes goes out of his way to indicate precisely how the white community controls the God concept within a legal framework. For instance, on the night of the performance, when the black players are supposed to strike, God arrives at the theater in the nation's capital with a formidable escort: "God arrived with motorcycle cops in front of his car. He had come a little early to address the cast. With him was the white stage manager and a representative of the New York producing office" (124). In the political capital of the United States, accompanied by a representative of the economic capital of the United States, and escorted by official enforcers of the United States law, God arrives early to converse with the band of rebel angels. God's objective is to secure order; He is the basis and foundation of the political, economic, and legal system of the United States of America. To oppose the political, economic, or legal system, therefore, is to oppose God. It is to be a renegade angel, a Lucifer who must be cast into perdition. Important to note, of course, is that God is not a neutral and objective arbitrator of the law, even though He is supposed to appear as such. He is a puppet whose political, economic, and legal views are determined by those in power. Notice how "white men" are frequently "accompanying God" (125). Guarded by "two [white] detectives" (124), God lays down the law. This explains why the narrator refers to God as an "Uncle Tom" (124).

But laying down the law does not just mean producing an external legal statute that all people must accept. It means structuring subjects at the level of desire; it means politically and legally orienting people toward themselves, others, and the world. This violent construction of the subject at the level of desire accounts for the poignant and disturbing conclusion of "Trouble with the Angels." With God's authorization, the two white detectives can legally arrest Logan. But notice, while the conclusion mentions Logan, who is crying as he is being taken to jail, it focuses mainly on the emotional orientation of the actors: "Most of the actors *wanted* to think Logan was crying because he was being arrested—but in their souls they knew that was not why he wept" (125). The actors, who have been constructed at the level of desire through God's declaration, desire to think that Logan weeps because he has been arrested. And Logan would have good reason to cry, because he has recently become a father and "so he needed to hold his job as a singing angel" (122). By getting arrested, Logan would lose his job and therefore be unable to feed his family. Such is what the actors wanted to think is the reason for Logan's tears.

But at a deeper level, a level more profound than their constructed desire, they know that their obvious surface explanation of the tears is inadequate. ("in their souls they know that was not why he wept"). Up to this point, Logan has resisted allowing God to structure him as a desiring subject. While the players have allowed God to construct them such that they willingly desire their own dehumanization, their own inequality before the God-sanctioned law, Logan has rejected God and his law. Consequently, Logan is, at the level of desire, an outlaw, a renegade who threatens not just a specific law but Law itself. In his discussion of the criminal, Derrida explains why someone like Logan both fascinates and terrifies: "The admiring fascination exerted on the people by 'the figure of the "great" criminal' . . . can be explained as follows: it is not someone who has committed this or that crime for which one feels a secret admiration; it is someone who, in defying the law, lays bare the violence of the legal system, the juridical order itself" ("Force" 33). In western culture, the God concept has been consistently invoked in order to justify the existence of a neutral, objective, and legitimate source of justice. But for Hughes, the God concept is the most effective instrument for constructing desiring subjects such that they willingly accept degrading and dehumanizing laws as neutral, objective, and legitimate. Such is the experience the players have undergone. Through God's *authorizing* pronouncement, the thespians accept and even support a law that denies them equality and dignity. By rejecting God's sanctioned laws and by opposing the theologically grounded legal apparatus, Logan does more than just defy a legal statute and demonstrate that he has not allowed God to construct him as a desiring subject. He has implicitly exposed the originary "violence of the legal system, the juridical order itself."

In essence, God is not a neutral, objective, and just Being who neutrally, objectively, and justly discloses Himself and His laws to neutral, objective, and just believers. To the contrary, God is a concept that becomes through psychic violence, a violence that brings desiring subjects into being such that they willingly accept and desire the rule of Law, even when specific laws sanction their own dehumanization and degradation. The thespians desire God's law, not because it is a pregiven Truth that neutrally and objectively represents societal justice (though they think so), but because they have been violently constructed, at the level of desire, to see and experience themselves, others, and the world through the lens of the God-puppet's law, a God-puppet who serves the interests and needs of the white community. By opposing God and His laws, Logan implicitly exposes the psychic violence that has been done to the players in and through God. In essence, his act of defiance exposes the external legal statute and the internally constructed desire as a violently grounded rule of law, which is established at the cost of "race pride, decency, or elementary human rights."

So what do his final tears signify? The God-sanctioned legal apparatus is overwhelmingly powerful, so psychologically and culturally thorough and complete that resistance is nearly impossible. When the detectives arrest Logan, the players realize, on the surface, that he will lose his job and be unable to support his family. Such is the interpretation they desire in order to explain the tears. But on a deeper level, they realize that the Hound of Heaven has finally got Logan, that Logan will now be brought into psychological being, at the level of desire, as a God-determined, law-abiding citizen. This experience is the worst thing that could happen. To be sure, being arrested will do serious damage to Logan's family (he will not be able to support his family), but becoming an obedient servant of the Lord will seriously damage the entire black community. Logan's resistance to God is based on his desire to fight "prejudice" and to buck "against the traces of discrimination and Jim Crow" (122). But once he is arrested, once he is drawn into the God-law machinery, he will be constructed, at the level of desire, to accept and even support the God-sanctioned laws. What this means for the black community is the loss of a powerful voice of resistance, a voice that could potentially counteract the emotional and psychological conditioning of black folk in relation to degrading and dehumanizing laws. At their deepest level, the players know that Logan realizes that he will now become one of them, a servant of the Lord who will say that God is right and, in so doing, willingly accept laws that sanction their own dehumanization and degradation. This is why Logan weeps, and the players, at their deepest level, know this.

In short, the God concept leads to alienation, according to Hughes. But there are two separate types of alienation. The first relates to the perpetrators of racist oppression. Let me turn to Hughes's 1927 story "The Young Glory of Him" to outline how this particular form of alienation functions. Central to this story is the suicide of Daisy Jones, a recent college graduate who is accompanying her white missionary parents to Africa. On board is Eric Gynt, a handsome sailor who takes considerable pride in his female sexual conquests. Indeed, he collects souvenirs from each woman he seduces. On the surface, this story is very simple. Naïve and inexperienced, Daisy falls in love with the womanizer, Eric, who quickly seduces and then dumps her. When Daisy realizes that Eric does not love her, she commits suicide. As for Eric, he initially regrets his behavior, but after a few days, he is "all right again, laughing, singing, joking, and swearing as usual" (102). The story ends with Eric returning to his old self, as he takes "the little black Bible that had once belonged to Daisy Jones" and stores it alongside "a garter from Horta, a red silk stocking from New York, a jeweled dagger from Havana, and a bunch of flaxen curls that a girl in Copenhagen gave him" (16).

Readers unaware of Hughes's subsurface complexity could easily interpret this story as a simple indictment of the ruthless behavior of a privileged white European male, behavior consistent with those who regularly traveled to Africa to exploit its people and resources. But actually this story is a complex examination of the psychology of missionaries, those who seemingly love the infidels to whom they bring the Good News. Hughes invites his reader to think critically about the "well-meaning middle-aged New England missionaries" at the end of the first section of the story. What we learn of Daisy's missionary parents is that they "had been stationed in Africa" for ten years "and only once in all this time had they returned to America to see Daisy" (11). There is clearly a lack of connection and warmth between Daisy and her parents, which results in awkward interactions. To make matters worse, the parents, without even knowing their daughter, want to decide her vocation: "They didn't know her very well, they said. She had always been away from them, but they hoped to make a missionary of her, too" (11). The lack of motivation to see their daughter, the cold and distant relationship, the attempt to decide their daughter's future without really knowing her—these things certainly do not give the reader a favorable impression of the missionaries.

But what ultimately casts the missionaries in a very negative light is a conversation they have with a trader who is also traveling to Africa. After the captain of the ship tells Daisy's parents that they are doing "good work" in Africa, the trader agrees. In the next sentence, however, the conversation shifts to the need to outdo Catholic missionaries: "Then the missionaries and the trader began a conversation concerning the necessity for more Christian Protestant missions along the Congo in order to combat the spread of Catholicism" (11). On the surface, the putative motivation for establishing a Christian mission in the Congo would be salvation and love. Given that Africans are God's people, the missionaries, who love all people and therefore want to bring God's love to them, would best fulfill their Christian duty by bringing the true Word of God to the benighted Africans. But in their discussion with the trader (significantly, a man who earns a living by locating and exchanging commodities), the missionaries unwittingly disclose their true motivation for bringing the Gospel to the Congo. Their driving passion is not love of the Africans; it is not care and concern for the quality of the Africans' lives or their personal or communal happiness. Rather, they, like the trader, collect goods. Traders and missionaries alike are scrambling to Africa to amass commodities in the name of nation and religion. So just as King Leopold II ordered scores of traders to colonize Africa in order to bolster the position of Belgium in the global marketplace, so too have Protestant Churches ordered scores of missionaries to convert Africa in order to bolster the position of Protestantism in the global religious place. Colonizers and missionaries are ultimately governed by the same motivation.

Of course, readers of this story could easily object that this one conversation between the trader and the couple is not nearly enough to justify such a critical interpretation of the missionaries. But my interpretation does not hinge on this single passage. In this story, Hughes draws a very clear parallel between Eric and the missionaries in order to identify the central energy animating their relationship to the commodities that they collect. The story ends with Eric collecting souvenirs from his conquests, people like Daisy who thought that Eric loved them. In like manner, the first section of the story concludes with the missionaries collecting Africans like souvenirs, people who may have accepted the missionaries' surface rhetoric of love. In both cases, love effectively conceals the subsurface motivation of collecting objects in order to expand and energize their national or religious base. So instead of being unified with the objects of their seeming love, both Eric and the missionaries are ultimately alienated from them.

Let me detail more precisely the nature of this alienation. Eric does not spend time trying to understand Daisy's inner life, her needs, abilities, and desires. He has a personal agenda, which is to amass as many souvenirs from his commodified victims as possible: "I got a box of souvenirs, and letters, and pictures from damn near every girl I ever knew anywhere" (12), Eric boasts to his comrades (12). What is of central importance is Eric's stature among his shipmates. The more women he seduces, the more souvenirs he acquires from his conquests, the more he will increase his aura of superiority and privilege. But his success presupposes a deep level of alienation from his victims. Instead of getting to know Daisy's inner life, and then modifying his behavior in order to accommodate *her* needs and desires, Eric bases his behavior solely on his own objectives.

But what is so striking about Eric's treatment of Daisy is his strategic use of love as a method for concealing his true objective, a method that serves to alienate him even further from her. The first level of alienation involves strategically ignoring the interests, needs, and desires of the targeted person, an alienation based on disregard. The second level of alienation involves deception. To seduce the targeted person, seducers must effectively conceal the unsavory objective of collecting people in order to increase the aura of their nation or religion. To this end, the concept of love is invaluable. Indeed, nothing can more effectively conceal a reprehensible motive than love. But to use love to conceal a subsurface motivation ensures a complete alienation. With the first type of alienation, the perpetrator disregards the interests, needs, and desires of the targeted person, whereas with the second type of alienation, the perpetrator uses a sophisticated device to conceal a ruthless subsurface motivation. So when Daisy discovers that Eric really does not love her, she feels alienated at two levels. First, Eric has not understood, appreciated, or taken into account her deepest needs and desires. Second, he has manipulated her by using a sophisticated system of love to conceal his unsavory objective.

This two-tiered alienation theory effectively illuminates the way the missionaries relate to their subjects/victims. For instance, we see how the missionaries alienate even their own daughter by ignoring what is most meaningful to her. As I have already mentioned, the missionaries certainly do not have a warm or intimate relationship with their daughter, so instead of making a judgment about her future on the basis of her needs, interests, and desires, they, like Eric, make a decision based on their own objective. Their personal agenda leads them to disregard Daisy's inner life, and, as a consequence, like Eric, all three of them alienate her.

While the story does not directly give us an example of the missionaries alienating people through deception, it certainly invites us, through a parallel-construction narrative device, to think of the missionaries' relationship to the Africans in these terms. What we know of victims, like Daisy, is that they ultimately discover that the surface rhetoric of love, which has been used to seduce them, turns out to be false: "I thought he loved me, but I know he doesn't. I can't bear it" (16). For Eric, it has been the desire to collect another female conquest that has motivated him to get involved with Daisy. When Daisy discovers Eric's subsurface motivation, she is devastated, which leads to her experience of alienation. While we never see the missionaries interacting with Africans in this story, we do see their subsurface motivation for bringing Christ to the natives—they are collecting souls, just as Eric collects women. Through this clear parallel, Hughes is inviting us to draw the logical conclusions. Just as Eric uses a surface rhetoric of love to seduce Daisy, so too have the missionaries used a surface rhetoric of love to seduce the Congolese. But just as Daisy experiences profound alienation once she discovers the subsurface motivation of Eric's behavior, so too would the Congolese experience profound alienation once they discover the subsurface motivation of the missionaries' behavior. Of course, what would differentiate Eric from the missionaries is his level of consciousness. While Eric admits that his true motive is to collect souvenirs from unsuspecting women, the missionaries would never admit to themselves or others that their true motive for converting Africans is to collect members in order to outdo Catholics. And yet the logic of this story suggests that the missionaries' motivation is identical to Eric's, and as a consequence we can infer that many Africans would have experienced the same kind of alienation as Daisy: "We thought they [the missionaries] loved us, but we know they don't. We can't bear it." As with Daisy in relation to Eric, the Congolese would discover that the missionaries do not have a genuine interest in their personal well-being.

Now let us look at alienation insofar as it affects victims of theistic systems. While "The Young Glory of Him" examines the psychology of oppressor theists, specifically insofar as their Gospel of Love functions to alienate witting and unwitting perpetrators from their victims, "Trouble With the Angels" examines the psychology of oppressed theists, specifically insofar as the God concept functions to alienate victims from themselves. The God concept functions to alienate the African Americans of "Trouble With the Angels" on two levels. First, the post-God "human" comes into being, as Fanon suggests (see section five of chapter 1), the moment it takes its "humanity," the moment it activates itself as a "self"-naming, "self"-constituting, "self"-creating agent. However, the God concept, which justifies the existence of a pregiven Law, makes such an experience of "self" impossible.

Let me explain why. By internalizing, at the level of desire, the view that God is right, the black thespians have accepted the Law. By Law I do not mean any individual law, like a Jim Crow law or a biological law of nature. Rather, I am referring to Law as a pregiven condition of possibility that, like God, would exist even were there no humans to "discover" it. Such Law is the foundation for individual laws; it is the condition under which specific laws have legitimacy. Given the existence of such a Law, to come into contact with one's self, to realize within one's self the Law of Justice and Justice as Law, one must submit to the Law, the Eternal God-inscribed Law that Theseus of Sophocles'

Antigone failed to understand but that Antigone understood all too well. In this system, Law is a pregiven Reality that makes individual laws possible. From this perspective, for individuals to connect themselves to themselves, they must begin the process of Self-knowledge and Self-actualization by accepting and affirming the existence of a pregiven Law.

What the God-inscribed Law philosophy entails is a human nature that is what it is whether humans perceive it or not. Humans have a nature or essence that must be discovered and accurately represented. The epistemological task, therefore, is to discover the Law in relation to a human's being. "Self"-creation, "self"-definition, "self"-construction become nonsensical and absurd in such a world. Indeed, should individuals construct themselves in opposition to the law of their being, the law that there is a Law that is the precondition for the existence of individual laws, they would alienate themselves from themselves. To avoid alienation, therefore, individuals must harmonize their vision of themselves with the pregiven Law. And since God is the author of the Law, to oppose it is to oppose God. Within the context of "Trouble With the Angels," once God is right, to be right with God, one must accept God's pregiven Law. To question the existence of the Law or to oppose it would result—necessarily—in alienation from Self.

If, however, we think of the "human" as a being that actualizes itself only insofar as it creates itself, then the pregiven God/Law model of subjectivity would function to alienate individuals from themselves. This is the case because the two divergent approaches prioritize different intellectual capacities for human self-actualization. According to the God/Law model, knowledge as discovery is crucial, which means that, once individuals understand that Law is the primordial password to the Self, then acceptance of and submission to the pregiven Law is the road to inner harmony. According to the constructionist model, knowledge as psychosemiotic creation is crucial, which means that, once individuals understand that "law" is a human-constructed concept, then humans will experience fulfillment only insofar as they take an active role in the construction of the "law," whether it is the law of the land or the law of their being.

With regard to the black thespians of "Trouble With the Angels," instead of thinking of the "law" as something that they, in conjunction with other interested groups, construct in relation to their communal interests, needs, and desires, they fatalistically accept the Eternal and Immutable Law. The very acceptance of such a Law renders the creative construction of "law" futile. So at the level of desire, the players cede their right and desire to construct the law of the land and the law of their being. After all, there is no need to construct such a law, since it has been created even before they came into being. Furthermore, to engage in the construction of the law would be to defy God. Given these two prohibitive factors, which function to alienate the players from their desire to create themselves as ontological equals of whites, it should come as no surprise that the players really did not want to strike—to strike would be to oppose not just a law but Law itself, that which is pregiven in and through God.

Therefore, by accepting the God/Law model, the African American players alienate themselves; they desire obedience and submission to Law, which makes them renounce their capacity to become self-determining agents who create the law of the land and the law of their own being. But they alienate themselves in a very local and specific sense as well. In short, they have renounced their capacity to create their world and themselves. In practical terms, instead of creating "laws" that adequately represent the needs, desires, and interests of their people, the African Americans simply accept that God is right. And since God is so clearly a puppet controlled by the white folk, in submitting to God, the black players are submitting to them. Accepting God, therefore, means the loss of agency, the agency of self-construction.

In addition to alienating themselves by renouncing their creative faculty, they also alienate themselves by internalizing specific laws that deny black folk access to the cultural resources that empower and foster growth and development. In "Trouble With the Angels," the Jim Crow law obviously undermines "race pride, decency, or elementary human rights." But more than that, by accepting, at the level of desire, that the law is right, the players willingly deprive fellow African Americans of the opportunity to hear black spirituals, to see black performers, and to watch a black play. In essence, the law functions to alienate everyday black folk from the aesthetic forms of their own community, the very forms that expose the structures of oppression, that celebrate black achievement, and that inspire individuals "to strive, to seek, to find, and not to yield." By making such an experience for African Americans scarce, the white community would effectively limit the revolutionary fervor that poignant art so often inspires.

Additionally, internalizing the Jim Crow law means alienating themselves from their desire for equality and dignity. This is most obviously the case in that the law prohibits blacks from attending the play. Whatever desire blacks may have for equal treatment before the law, they must deny it. It also means alienating themselves from the desire to play an active role in the body politic.

If they are not worthy of attending a play performed by black players, then how would they be worthy of making a political contribution? The acknowledgment that "God is right" has ultimately alienated African Americans from themselves at almost every level possible. Such is the reason why Hughes consistently treats the puppet God as a being that has ultimately done incalculable damage to the black community.

5

Touchstone Narratives

Measuring the Political Value of the God Concept

"Anyhow, I say, the God I been praying and writing to is a man. And act just like all the other mens I know. Trifling, forgitful and lowdown."

Alice Walker, *The Color Purple*

Let me briefly summarize what I have argued up to this point. In the first chapter, I examined the epistemological/ontological recursive loop of theology, which enables those who control the God concept to ontologize themselves as fully human. Through this unassailable system, the culture's designated superiors can control the intellectual means of production, which means that they can define themselves and others, while those who do not control the intellectual means of production can only be defined. In chapter 2, I examined how this recursive loop, which is nearly impossible to deconstruct, functions to divest culturally designated inferiors of agency over their bodies. In chapter 3, I examined how theists, once they are inscribed within the recursive loop, make use of rapelike violence in their effort to coerce infidels into making a faith declaration. In chapter 4, I examined how the God concept functions in the political formation of individual laws and the Law. Moreover, I examined how, once the God concept has been established as the basis and foundation of laws and the Law, a fatalism settles into the bodies of culturally designated inferiors.

Alone, each of these theories has limited value, but taken together, they yield an extremely complex view of the sociocultural dynamics of faith, specifically insofar as those dynamics legitimize a massive system of exploitation and degradation that could not function or even exist without the God concept. Nowhere are these dynamics more intelligently examined than in a newly emerging genre of writing, which I call Touchstone narratives. Touchstone narratives have their origin in the conversion story. As Edward Morgan has argued, there is a certain formula to the conversion narrative, what he refers to as the "morphology of conversion" (66–73). According to the standard conversion story, the tale begins with a person steeped in mortal sin and spiritual ignorance. Next, through contact with enlightened believers or through a direct encounter with "God," the heathen accepts the spiritual truth and renounces his/her old life. The final part of the narrative documents the soul's spiritual progression, while it simultaneously justifies the superiority of those who live in communion with God. This last part of the story is linked with the text's attempt to evangelize.

Instead of chronicling the conversion of the writer, Touchstone narratives document the reasons why African American atheists reject the God concept and religion. A touchstone is used to determine the quality or value of something. But the particular Touchstone that I have in mind is the character from Shakespeare's brilliant play *As You Like It*. Surrounded by figures who can see more devils than vast Hell can hold, Touchstone functions to temper the overheated imagination. So when Rosalind, who is smitten with Orlando, discovers Orlando's trite love sonnets, Touchstone produces his own verse:

If a hart do lack a hind,
Let him seek out Rosalind.
If the cat will after kind,
So be sure will Rosalind. (3.2.106–10)

Dashing off this impromptu rhyme serves as a word of caution to the credulous—any fool can produce unheroic couplets. Not surprisingly, in her encounters with her future lover, Rosalind puts Orlando's love to the test. The cynical and skeptical Touchstone has had his effect: he forces characters to interrogate the legitimacy of seductive discourses. But more than that, he consistently deflates hyperbolic assertions, forcing characters to honestly appraise their emotions and ideas. Writers like Langston Hughes, Zora Neale Hurston, Richard Wright, and J. Saunders Redding produce Touchstone narratives, but what they put to the test is the God concept. And their conclusion is that God is an idea that should probably be put to rest.[1]

To understand what led these writers to this conclusion, we must first make a crucial distinction between eighteenth- and nineteenth- versus twentieth-century approaches to the God concept. As has been well documented, white American Christians subjugated and violated nonwhites, Christian or not, with tenacious regularity for centuries, but for pre-twentieth-century African American Christians, this brutal treatment, while heinous, did not lead many to renounce the faith. The reason: they had internalized an intellectual framework that enabled them to distinguish the true faith, which would never sanction violence, abuse, and/or injustice, from the erring practitioners of the faith, whose reprehensible behavior was considered out of step with the true faith.

To indicate more precisely how this pure-Christianity/erring-practitioner model functioned, let me briefly discuss three very important and influential pre-twentieth-century life-writing narratives. In his autobiography, Frederick Douglass explicitly condemns the "slaveholding religion" (326) of the United States, boldly claiming that Christianity, especially in the South, "is a mere covering for the most horrid crimes,—a justifier of the most appalling barbarity,—a sanctifier of the most hateful frauds,—and a dark shelter under which the darkest, foulest, grossest, and most infernal deeds of slaveholders find the strongest protection" (301). At this point, Douglass is not just suggesting that southern Christians were—coincidentally—vicious slaveholders. He actually notes that there is a causal link between Christianity and "the most horrid crimes," for once his master, Captain Auld, experienced a religious conversion, he became "more cruel and hateful in all his ways" (287). As Douglass notes: "Prior to his conversion, he [Auld] relied upon his own depravity to shield and sustain him in his savage barbarity; but after his conversion, he found religious sanction and support for his slaveholding cruelty" (287). Harriet Jacobs makes a similar observation after her master, Dr. Flint, joined the Episcopal Church. Like Douglass, she thought his declaration of faith would have "a purifying effect on the character" of her master, but what she discovered is that she suffered "the worst persecutions" from him "after he was a communicant" (326). In short, there seems to be a causal link between being a Christian and being a barbaric slaveholder. To quote Douglass: "Were I to be again reduced to the chains of slavery, next to that enslavement, I should regard being the slave of a religious master the greatest calamity that could befall me. For of all slaveholders with whom I have ever met, religious slaveholders are the worst" (301–2).

And yet Douglass insists in the appendix of his autobiography that there is a huge distinction between "the *slaveholding religion* of this land" and "Christianity proper" (326). Indeed, he suggests that the behavior of slaveholding Christians is so inconsistent with true Christianity that slaveholding Christians do not actually qualify as Christians: "I love the pure, peaceable, and impartial Christianity of Christ: I therefore hate the corrupt, slaveholding, women-whipping, cradle-plundering, partial and hypocritical Christianity of this land. Indeed, I can see no reason, but the most deceitful one, for calling the religion of this land Christianity" (326). For Douglass, there exists such a thing as "Christianity proper," which he knows and understands, and given this knowledge, southern slaveholding Christians are not really Christian because they fail to meet the true definition. Therefore, instead of faulting Christianity for the horrors of slavery, even though there are many passages in the Bible that support slavery and none that clearly condemn it, he only faults the erring practitioners of the faith. Such an implicit distinction is at work in *The Life of Olaudah Equiano*. For instance, after watching a number of people being sold into slavery, Equiano interjects: "O, ye nominal Christians! might not an African ask you, 'learned you this from your God, who says unto you, Do unto all men as you would men should do unto you?'" (38). Given Christ's Golden Rule, which for Equiano trumps the Bible's slavery passages, slaveholding Christians implicitly violate the Golden Rule. Therefore, instead of rejecting Christianity for sanctioning slavery, Equiano faults hypocritical Christians, those who fail to conform their lives to the True Faith.

By the twentieth century, when intellectuals in many disciplines began to conclude that knowledge is psychosemiotic construction rather than a pregiven reality, African American religious life-writing underwent a radical transformation. Instead of distinguishing pure religion from its erring practitioners, these writers developed a theory of knowledge that made such a distinction both untenable and incoherent. For these writers, even if there were such a thing as a pure Christianity or a pure religion, they would contend that the human, governed as it is by subjective interests and steeped in its culture's ideology, would be incapable of determining whether it was in epistemological possession of the true faith or not. But more than that, these writers started to conclude that there is no such thing as a pure ideal. Rather, they entertained the idea that positing the existence of a pure ideal was the dominant political power's most effective ideological instrument for warding off criticism and instituting an oppressive politics. For the atheists in this study, God is an anthropomorphic projection that assumes a provisional form in and through a specific discourse. Therefore, the God concept is whatever the believers happen to believe it to be, and since God has been consistently used as a weapon to perpetuate the wicked idea of human inferiority, these writers reject the God concept.

"Before I had been made to go to church, I had given God's existence a sort of tacit assent, but after having seen His creatures serve Him at first hand, I had had my doubts."

Richard Wright, *Black Boy*

To express their objection to the God concept, these writers forged the Touchstone narrative. And just as there is a morphology to the conversion narrative, so too is there a morphology to the Touchstone narrative. In my studies of these narrative forms, I have been able to identify four stages. The first consists of the apostate's acknowledgment that he or she has not been able to take the leap of faith. Next, the religious community tries to convert the erring infidel. After undergoing a harrowing experience at the hands of the community of believers, the apostate emphatically rejects the God concept. The final and most significant stage is the writer's analysis of the destructive personal and political consequences of religious belief.

In the first stage, when the writer openly or tacitly acknowledges that he or she has not yet been able to take the leap of faith, there is generally little hostility toward God or the religious community. For instance, in *The Big Sea*, the twelve-year-old Langston Hughes, who had not yet made a declaration of faith, admits that he was predisposed in favor of God, for all his elders told him that, once converted, a person "could see and hear and feel Jesus" in his or her "soul" (19). Eager and open-minded, Hughes went to a revival meeting to wait "for Jesus to come" to him. Sitting on the mourners' bench, watching his peers turn to Christ, the young Hughes "kept waiting to *see* Jesus." At this point, Hughes neither believes nor disbelieves; he simply waits for something to give him justification for believing. But that something never materializes: "Nothing! I wanted something to happen to me; but nothing happened" (20).

In *Dust Tracks on a Road*, Zora Neale Hurston confesses that, even though she grew up in a preacher's home, she had questioned religious belief from as early as she could remember (193). Hurston's picture of her father's Missionary Baptist Church is respectful and endearing. The community of believers nods "with conviction in time to" her father's words (193) and some speak "of sights and scenes around God's throne" (194). Hurston confesses that she "enjoyed participation [in the church services] at times," but she qualifies the nature of her participation by saying that she "was moved, not by the spirit, but by action, more or less dramatic" (195). Unlike the faithful, Hurston cannot accept the simple religious answers to life's most perplexing questions. Moreover, when she observes the way believers live and behave, she notes that "these people looked and acted like everybody else." Believing in God certainly does nothing to make people any better than anyone else. Therefore, Hurston concludes that she simply could not utter a declaration "of love for a being that nobody could see" (195).

Richard Wright documents how, before being subtly pressured to accept Christ, he had neither positive nor negative feelings about God. After one of his classmates introduces the topic of salvation, Wright confesses: "I had not settled in my mind whether I believed in God or not; His existence or nonexistence never worried me" (*Black Boy* 115). While Wright seems to be somewhat agnostic at this point, he then goes on to claim that, before he had been forced to attend church, he "had given God's existence a sort of tacit assent" (115). Being critical of God or His believers simply did not come into question for the young Wright.

J. Saunders Redding fulfills the requirement of the first stage of the Touchstone narrative, but he is not nearly as detailed as the others. When he pronounces himself an unbeliever, he admits that he does not know how long he has "held both God and the Christian religion in some doubt, though it must have been since [his] teens" (138). Redding considers his inability to believe inexplicable, since his father was "very religious, of great and clear and unbending faith," while his mother would sometimes be "so deeply touched by a religious feeling that she could not keep back the tears" (138). Consistent with the other three writers, Redding admits that he cannot believe, but he also exhibited no antipathy for God or religion when he was young.

It is during the second stage of the Touchstone narrative, which consists of the community of believers using ruthless and vicious tactics to convert the infidel, that the writer begins to turn against God and religion. What these writers experience can only be described as a psychological gang rape, something akin to what Helga Crane undergoes in Larsen's *Quicksand* (see chapter 3). In *The Big Sea*, the communal violation commences with the preacher's "wonderful rhythmical sermon," which is punctuated with "moans and shouts and lonely cries and pictures of hell" (19). This is enough to terrify at least a few to jump up and go "to Jesus right away." But for a hardened twelve-year-old sinner like Hughes and his friend Westley, a promised future in the fiery abyss is not enough to inspire the two to embrace Christ. So the community must apply more pressure, this time sending a "great many old people" to kneel around the sinful youth and to hover over them praying. This succeeds in extracting a declaration from Westley but not from Hughes. Alone, unable to believe, and terrified, the young Hughes contemplates his situation. But as he does so, his aunt joins the crowd of elders, kneels, and cries, "while prayers and songs" (20) swirl around the boy. When this does not succeed, the whole congregation sends up a prayer "in a mighty wail of moans and voices" (20). All of this external pressure leads Hughes to renounce the desires of his will and to make a declaration of faith. The community has won. Through a strategically coordinated effort in psychological manipulation and coercion, it has enacted its own will and desire on the body of the child.

But the victory is short-lived, for when the young Hughes returns home, he cannot hold back his tears. His aunt interprets his crying as a sign that "the Holy Ghost had come into [his] life" and that he "had seen Jesus," but Hughes discloses the real reason for his tears: "I was really crying because I couldn't bear to tell her that I lied, that I had deceived everybody in the church, that I hadn't seen Jesus, and that now I didn't believe there was a Jesus any more, since he didn't come to help me" (21). This simple rejection of Christianity, which fulfills the third requirement of the Touchstone narrative, is far more radical than one might initially assume. Equiano, Douglass, and Jacobs make a distinction between hypocritical Christians and true Christianity, so while they all feel comfortable faulting erring practitioners of the faith, they neither criticize nor reject Christianity as such—they certainly could not have said that they "didn't believe there was a Jesus any more." Based on his experience with the Christian community, however, Hughes rejects Christianity as such, which means saying "Goodbye Christ."

This new development is hugely significant because it reflects a shift in the culture's thinking about knowledge. The traditional view, that there exists a mind-independent truth that is best suited to signify the world aright, has more often than not presupposed that one of those truths consists of an ideal of justice, goodness, and righteousness, which Christianity incarnates. (For a more detailed examination of this theory of knowledge, see chapter 2.) So when Christians misbehave, they do so either because they have failed to understand true Christianity or they have conducted themselves, whether they know it or not, in an un-Christian manner. Given that Christianity incarnates the mind-independent ideal, Equiano, Jacobs, and Douglass reject perverted versions of Christianity but never Christianity as such. By contrast, the writers who produce Touchstone narratives reject both the assumption that there exists a mind-independent truth and that Christianity embodies any kind of ideal. What these writers maintain is that all ideals (like Christianity) consist of "our own conceptions of what things are," to quote Wright's Cross Damon, a view that is totally consistent with Hughes's view of the gods as mere puppets at the beck and call of those in positions of power. What motivates these writers to reject the idea of a truth is the way this untainted ideal leads people to treat certain institutions of power as inviolable. Put more concretely, holding the view that there exists an ideal and that Christianity embodies that ideal prohibits anyone from questioning whether Christianity has been the source of injustice. Within the context of the African American writers who have discussed religion in their autobiographies, Hughes's decision to collapse the distinction between erring practitioners of the faith and true Christianity introduces a new way of thinking about Christianity. Specifically, it leads him to reject Christianity altogether. Not surprisingly, Hurston, Wright, and Redding, who had all read Hughes's autobiography, pick up where he left off.

Hurston's second-stage encounter does not occur, as it does for Hughes and Wright, in the church but in a conversation with her preacher father and two of his colleagues. After questioning the logic of Christian concepts like redemption and resurrection, Hurston learns a valuable lesson about challenging the faith or expressing her doubt: "When they got through with me, I knew better than to say that out loud again, but their shocked and angry tirades did nothing for my bewilderment. My head was full of misty fumes of doubt" (194). Larsen's dramatization of the believers' rapelike violence against infidels sheds some light on John Hurston's violent treatment of his daughter. As I argued in the Larsen chapter, believers distinguish the relative matters of the ephemeral world from the absolute matters of the spiritual world. Because believers can see what infidels cannot, namely, the human's deepest spiritual needs and desires, they feel that they have not only a right but also an obligation to coerce infidels into accepting a true spiritual perspective. To that end, they are spiritually, though not legally, authorized to use whatever means necessary, including physical or psychological violence, to exact a declaration of belief from the infidel. So when John Hurston and his colleagues launch into their "shocked and angry tirades," they would feel more than justified in applying such "pressure on the unconverted" (196).

To underscore the violent nature of this act of pressuring the unconverted into the faith, Hurston strategically segues from the experiences in her father's church to the history of Christianity. The implication is that the psychological violence and abuse that Hurston experiences at the hands of her father has its origins in the religious tradition to which he belongs. For instance, after mentioning that she "studied the history of the great religions of the world" (200), she discusses the emperor Constantine's conversion to Christianity, specifically how his sudden transformation led him "to win a great battle" and "to start out on his missionary journey with his sword." Just in case her reader may not want to draw a parallel between John Hurston and Constantine, Hurston makes the point explicitly: "He [Constantine] probably did not even have a good straining voice like my father to win converts and influence people. But he had his good points—one of them being a sword— and a seasoned army." To further draw a link between the large-scale military violence of Constantine and the psychological violence of the American Christian Church, Hurston uses American colloquial expressions to describe Constantine's trek through Europe: "It seems that Reverend Brother Emperor Constantine carried the gospel up and down Europe with his revival meetings to such an extent that Christianity really took on." Calling Constantine "Reverend Brother" and dubbing his military conquests "revival meetings" is clearly an attempt to liken the Roman dictator to her father ("Reverend Jno" [193]), who would let himself go at revival meetings (195). But such a link can only have negative connotations for John Hurston, for as Zora makes clear, Constantine's success, like John's, has been based on violence: "Christianity was on its way to world power that would last. That was only the beginning. Military power was to be called in time and time again to carry forward the gospel of peace. There is not apt to be any difference of opinion between you and a dead man" (201). Just as John Hurston would silence his daughter for having a "difference of opinion," so too would Constantine silence anyone who differed with him. The strategic parallels between John Hurston and Constantine suggest that, while times have changed, Christians in the twentieth century make use of a similar type of violence for the same reasons as the fourth-century emperor. The violence in the twentieth century may be more psychological than physical, but the purpose and the effects are similar.

Given that religion involves a rapelike violence against the unconverted, it should come as no surprise that Hurston fulfills the third stage of the Touchstone narrative by rejecting God. She makes two separate declarations of unbelief. First, life is both difficult and unpredictable, so Hurston understands why humans feel that they must create an omnipotent being "to bolster up their feeling of weakness" (201). But Hurston notes that "the omnipotence" these people "rely upon is a creature of their own minds" and not an ontological reality. People believe not because there is a God but because they need to feel secure in a very insecure world. This need leads to the second reason for creating the God concept. Religions codify belief through their creeds, but as Hurston observes, "organized creeds are collections of words around a wish" (202). People do not submit to a religious creed because they have any evidence or justification for such belief. Rather, their creed, which is nothing more than wish-fulfillment, makes them see the world as they so desire. Such a view can only distort the world, so Hurston, who accepts the universe as she finds it and bows to its laws, concludes that she has no need either to rely upon a God-"creature" of her own mind or a religious institution.

Within the genre of Touchstone narratives, Wright provides one of the most horrific pictures of the community of believers as a band of gang rapists. Like Hurston, Wright claims that belief is all about control and dominance: "Wherever I found religion in my life I found strife, the attempt of one individual or group to rule another in the name of God. The naked will to power seemed always to walk in the wake of a hymn" (*Black Boy* 136). What concerns Wright most, however, is the way belief functions simultaneously to empower and to debilitate individuals. Through conversion, the community can establish an intense bond. For instance, as a young boy who tries to convert the twelve-year-old Wright claims, belief will mean that the two would be "true brothers in Christ" (114). Invoking the Chosen People mentality, the boy tells Wright that if he accepts Christ, he can expect love and kindness, but if he doesn't, the consequences can be dire: "'If *you* are kind to Him, He is a kind God,' the boy said, 'but God will not look at you if you don't look at Him'" (115). For a marginalized group, there is strength in numbers, so the desire to convert the young Richard is essential in order to provide his community with a front of solidarity, what Hurston refers to as "an alliance with omnipotence to bolster up their feelings of weakness." Consequently, for someone to reject God poses a threat to the community. Indeed, Wright describes the religious community as a tribe that ensnares individuals: "We young men had been trapped by the community, the tribe in which we lived and of which we were a part. The tribe, for its own safety, was asking us to be at one with it" (153). To reject God, therefore, is to reject the community, which explains why Wright's grandmother responds so passionately to his apostasy: "She was the oldest member of her church and it would have been unseemly if the only grandchild in her home could not be brought to these important services; she felt that if I were completely remiss in religious conformity it would cast doubt upon the staunchness of her faith, her capacity to convince and persuade, or merely her ability to apply the rod to my backside" (111). Only through communal participation can the illusion of faith be maintained, and since the community's need for a feeling of security and empowerment depends upon many individuals' willingness to take the leap of faith, apostasy strikes not so much at the heart of God as it does at the heart of the community.

Given the profound psychological need of the community, especially a downtrodden community, to establish solidarity and security, there is no tactic that it will not use in order to enforce belief. For instance, because Wright refuses to believe, his grandmother tells the young apostate that his mother has been ill as a result of his "faithlessness" (103). When the family realizes that guilt will not lead Wright to make a declaration of faith, the entire family becomes "kind and forgiving" (113). But Wright realizes that this change in behavior is just a ploy, which leads him to "an even greater emotional distance from them" (113). The most devastating experience occurs when Wright is identified at a church meeting as a lost soul. Although Wright claims that he is familiar with all the techniques preachers use to convert people, he is horrified to discover that the community would exploit his relationship with his mother to force him to make a declaration of faith. Urging the mothers to embrace their children, "the preacher launched into a highly emotional and symbolic sermon, recounting how our mothers had given birth to us, how they had nursed us from infancy, how they tended us when we were sick, how they had seen us grow up, how they had watched over us, how they had always known what was best for us" (154). The young Wright realizes his predicament: "If I refused, it meant that I did not love my mother, and no man in that tight little black community had ever been crazy enough to let himself be placed in such a position." In other words, "the tribe was asking us whether we shared its feelings; if we refused to join the church, it was equivalent to saying no, to placing ourselves in the position of moral monsters."

This is the kind of violence that Helga experiences in *Quicksand*, a violence that succeeds, at least for a few years, in ensnaring her into the tribe of believers. But for Wright it has the exact opposite effect. As Wright concludes: "This business of saving souls had no ethics; every human relationship was shamelessly exploited" (154). Not surprisingly, Wright fulfills the third stage of the Touchstone narrative by declaring his lack of belief. As he says when discussing his experiences with fellow intellectuals who worked with him at the post office, "We believed that man should live by hard facts alone, and we had so long ago put God out of our minds that we did not even discuss Him" (285). Of course, this declaration would become the basis of his novel *The Outsider*, but within the context of *Black Boy* it is an important element in the African American atheist's placement within the intellectual tradition of the Touchstone narrative.

Because Redding does not remember when he became an atheist, he does not fulfill the second part of the Touchstone narrative, but he meets the third-stage requirement. In a passage that I discussed in chapter 1, Redding concludes: "I simply rejected religion. I rejected God" (144). What Redding, however, lacks in the second stage, he more than compensates for in the final stage.

The fourth stage of the Touchstone narrative, which consists of the African American atheist's sociocultural critique of faith, features the most daring comments and observations on religion and God. Indeed, so radical was Hurston's *Dust Tracks on a Road* that her most scathing remarks about God and religion were bowdlerized from the original 1942 version of the book. In this last section of my analysis, instead of considering each writer's sociocultural critique separate and alone, I will combine them in order to illuminate the central insights that make their work so audacious, insightful, and relevant. However, I will primarily use Hurston's bowdlerized chapter "Seeing the World as It Is" to focus my discussion.

Following Hughes's lead, Hurston refuses to make a distinction between erring practitioners of the faith and an idealized version of Christianity. Hurston sees in the Bible not pure ideals that ensure justice but bigotry and hatred, a massive system that sanctions political violence and oppression. To underscore this view of the Bible, Hurston begins with a comic but blistering analysis of the way the ancient Hebrews made use of the God concept to justify large-scale atrocities. Let me quote this long passage in whole, for it brilliantly identifies the very mind-set that African American atheists consistently consider so dangerous:

> The Old Testament is devoted to what was right and just from the viewpoint of the ancient Hebrews. All of their enemies were twenty-two carat evil. They, the Hebrews, were never aggressors. The Lord wanted His children to have a country full of big grapes and tall corn. Incidentally, while they were getting it, they might as well get rid of some trashy tribes that He never did think much of, anyway. With all of its figs and things, Canaan was their destiny. God sent somebody especially to tell them about it. If the conquest looked like bloody rape to the Canaanites, that was because their evil ways would not let them see a point which was right under their nose. So you had to drive it in under the ribs. King David, who invented the "protection" racket in those days before he was saved by being made king, was a great hero. He was a man after God's own heart, and was quite serviceable in helping God get rid of no-count rascals who were cluttering up the place. (244–45)

Notice how Hurston underscores "what was right and just" from a particular perspective. The ancient Hebrews, who are God's Chosen People, control the epistemological/ontological recursive loop. Given their capacity to know God's will, that which is "right and just," we can infer that they are ontologically superior—they must be endowed with a superior epistemological capacity that allows them to see what others cannot. Not surprisingly, God specifically tells the Hebrews that he favors them—he wants them "to have a country full of big grapes and tall corn." So the Hebrews are ontologically superior by virtue of their capacity to know God's spiritual truth and by virtue of God's special treatment of them.

The Hebrews' enemies, by contrast, are ontologically inferior ("no-count rascals," who are "twenty-two carat evil") for two reasons. First, because they do not have the capacity to know God's will ("their evil ways would not let them see a point which was right under their nose"), we can infer that they are ontologically inferior. Not surprisingly, God specifically tells the Hebrews that their enemies are "some trashy tribes that He never did think much of, anyway." Of course, the Hebrews' behavior may seem "like bloody rape to the Canaanites," but this interpretation is immediately dismissed, since it is the Hebrews who control the intellectual means of production. By controlling the epistemological/ontological recursive loop, the Hebrews can justify committing atrocities against the Canaanites with emotional, psychological, and legal impunity.

To disable the recursive loop of theology, African American atheists reject a theory of knowledge that presupposes the existence of a mind-independent, God-created idea and ideal and they do this for three reasons. The first relates to the distinction between the true versus the distorted versions of religion or God. Even if there were such a thing as a True Church, a True Religion, a True God, or a True Christianity, one would always be left with questions: How do we know that such a True Anything exists? Or, how do we know who has the true interpretation? This recalls Redding's key insight in *On Being Negro in America*. The God concept undergoes "subtle modifications" in relation to the environment and the culture's ideology, so God will change in relation to the cultures that create Him. To talk about a true God or a true concept is incoherent for Redding, as it is for Wright. This is the case because there are no mind-independent ideas. As Wright's Cross Damon puts this, we only have "our own conceptions of what things are," and since humans are driven by a narrow and limited set of ideological interests, needs, and desires, their knowledge systems must reflect such biases.

Similarly for Hurston, since needs and desires will always play a role in the construction of knowledge, she makes no such distinction between a phantom concept like an immutable God and a culture's distorted version of God. Her theory of knowledge, in fact, prohibits such a distinction. In her world, all we have are the human constructions of God, the creatures of our own mind. Such a view leads Hurston to call into question the dubious idea of an absolute justice: "It would be wishful thinking to be searching for justice in the absolute. People are not made so it will happen, because, from all I can see, the world is a whole family of Hurstons. It has always been a family of Hurstons, so it is foolish to expect any justice untwisted by the selfish hand" (244). As an example of justice twisted by selfish interest and motivation, Hurston encourages her readers to turn to the Bible. Just like the Old Testament, the New Testament is "biased" (245), governed by an egocentric ideology and driven by a "selfish hand." Since the authors of the Bible were biased and limited humans, the ideas therein must also be biased and limited. By rejecting the idea of a pure ideal like justice, whether that ideal is embodied in Christianity or the Bible, Hurston is therefore free to examine all ideas and institutions in order to see if they are the source of the culture's systems of oppression and injustice. This is something that Equiano, Jacobs, and Douglass could not do, for they all assumed the existence of a pregiven ideal, like True Religion, True Christianity, or a True God. So while they all were willing to fault hypocritical practitioners of the faith, they were not willing to question or challenge Christianity or the Bible. As is obvious from Hurston's scathing critique of the Bible, she is very willing to critique practitioners of the faith as well as the faith itself.

The second reason why African American atheists reject the existence of God-created ideals relates to the way the perceived existence of such ideals enables those who control the intellectual means of production either to differentiate the human from the subhuman or to stratify humanness. Hurston achieves her objective at this point through an extended analysis of the dominant powers that commit atrocities against culturally designated inferiors. But, most significantly, she identifies the Chosen People mentality of the Bible, which provides a model for determining who is not human, as the source that legitimizes such atrocities. As I have argued in chapters 1 and 2, humanness in the West has been defined on the basis of a "person's" capacity to access a pregiven truth, specifically a person's ability to know God or a metaphysical truth. Those who can access such truths either are full-fledged humans or they have achieved their "highest humanity," while those who cannot access such truths belong to the "lower breeds" or are "born half-ape[s]." For Hurston, it is the Judeo-Christian tradition's theory of knowledge which has made such human-differentiating systems possible.

For instance, since the ancient Hebrews were in an intimate and loving relationship with God, they were considered the Chosen People, full-fledged humans worthy of special privileges from God. Since the Canaanites lacked knowledge of God-created truths, they were not fully human, so the ancient Hebrews could annihilate them, sparing no one, without contradicting the commandment not to kill. With the coming of Christ, however, the Hebrews lost their former title as the Chosen People, which meant that they would no longer control the epistemological/ontological recursive loop. Not coincidentally, just as the Hebrews used the recursive loop to define the Canaanites as "no-count rascals," now Christians could define Jews as the subhuman evil ones: "the orthodox Jew became a manifest enemy of right" (245). With their ability to define themselves as ontologically superior and the Jews as ontologically inferior, Christians were able to sidestep both the Ten Commandments and Christ's Golden Rule and thereby justify slaughtering Jews in the same way that the Hebrews justified annihilating the Canaanites. Hurston's logic is clear at this point. If what the Canaanites experienced at the hands of the Hebrews seemed like "bloody rape to the Canaanites," that was because the Canaanites did not have the spiritual eyes to "see a point which was right under their nose." In like manner, if what the Jews experienced at the hands of Christians seemed like bloody rape to the Jews, that would be because the Jews did not have the spiritual eyes to "see a point which was right under their eyes." And what is that point? That God wants Christians to rule and control the most coveted lands ("a country full of big grapes and tall corn") and that He wants Christians to get rid of some of the "trashy" Jewish "tribes."

Hurston's devastating depiction of religion and God might seem gratuitous, but actually her purpose is to illuminate the political situation of the 1940s. Like Césaire, Fanon, Baldwin, and Wright, Hurston considers Hitler's political agenda as having its origin in the Judeo-Christian tradition, so if we would understand the structure of mind that made Hitler's totalitarian agenda possible, an analysis of the psychology of religious belief would be the best place to begin. What the Hebrews and the Christians have done to the Canaanites and the Jews, Europeans have done to Asia and Africa. Transitioning from her analysis of the biblical basis of colonization to then-contemporary instances of such colonization certainly underscores the structural similarities. But let us examine a few crucial passages in order to better understand the nature of these similarities.

Hurston explicitly links contemporary political and traditional religious systems in her analysis of democracy. In a discussion of an abstract ruler, who successfully conquers a foreign people by killing "enough of them to convince the rest that they ought to support him with their lives and labor," the ruler will eventually be hailed as a hero, the conquered people memorializing "him in unforgetting stone with the sacred tool of his conquest in his hand." It might seem that she is discussing the conquests of ancient Hebrews or a totalitarian regime at this point, but she concludes the paragraph with a remark about democracy: "Democracy, like religion, never was designed to make our profit less" (248). On the surface, religion and democracy are noble ideals, systems that seemingly ensure social justice and provide the conditions for human flourishing. But beneath the surface, both are ruthless systems that effectively justify the economic exploitation of vulnerable peoples and cultures.

To illustrate her point, Hurston asks her reader to imagine the British quartering "troops in France" and forcing "the French to work for them for forty-eight cents a week," while the British would take "more than a billion dollars a year out of France" (248–49). Such a situation seems ludicrous, and yet the "British Government," Hurston continues, "does just that in India, to the glory of the democratic way." Instead of being condemned as ruthless robber barons or moral monsters, they "are hailed as not only great Empire builders" but also "as leaders of civilization" (249). For Britain to be able to colonize and brutalize India with psychological and legal impunity, but not be able to do the same to France, there must be in place a psychological and political system that justifies such action. That system is the Chosen People mentality of the Bible, which is grounded on the God concept.

Therefore, what makes Hurston's imaginative analysis of Britain colonizing France belong in the same chapter as her discussion of the ancient Hebrews' conquest of the Canaanites is the structure of mind that enables both groups to dominate others with political and legal impunity. Hurston does not spend much time detailing that structure of mind in her discussion of the British colonization of India, but she does not need to, since the structure is the same one that the Hebrews deployed in order to justify their exploitation and colonization of the Canaanites. And since Hurston has already compared religion to democracy, it is clear that she is inviting her reader to link the two examples. But let me highlight just a couple of the important connections.

The Hebrews feel justified in colonizing and even annihilating the Canaanites, because the Hebrews, as God's Chosen People, are full-fledged people, which means that they have certain inalienable rights that must be respected. Because the Canaanites are not in an intimate and loving relationship with the one True God, they are not full-fledged humans ("no-count rascals"), and since nonhumans or subhumans do not have human rights, the Hebrews are free to violate the Canaanites with impunity.

To be sure, the Canaanites, who feel that the ancient Hebrews' treatment of them is nothing less than "bloody rape," would be within their right to ask: how do we know that the ancient Hebrews are actually in communication with God? It is possible, after all, that they have fabricated not just their relationship with God but the God concept altogether in order to justify their colonizing politics. Hurston certainly realizes that the Hebrews' portrayal of God is a "creature of their own minds"—she explicitly states that it is biased. But how could she expose the whole political structure, which is based on a theological model of knowledge, as dangerous and flawed? If we take her then-contemporary example of the British colonization of France and India, we might be able to offer an answer. If one Hebrew tribe (tribe #1) told another Hebrew tribe (tribe #2) that they (tribe #1) are in an intimate relationship with the one and only true God and that God wants them to colonize or even annihilate the infidel tribe (tribe #2), it would be possible for tribe #2 to retort that they are in an intimate relationship with the one and only true God. This example would not only underscore the arbitrary nature of the God concept but also highlight the dangers and injustice of laying claim to God. Such is the effect that Hurston's imaginative construction of Britain colonizing France should have on her reader. Europeans generally agree that they, who worship the one and only true God, have a God-given right to colonize foreign lands and, when necessary, to exterminate the infidels who refuse to submit. But Europeans have a tacit agreement that they, as Christians, are all equally human and therefore it is unlawful and unacceptable to apply a colonizing philosophy to fellow Europeans. So applying colonizing practices to France would be an egregious violation of the European sensibility, whereas applying them to India would not. Europeans have in place the exact same epistemological/ontological model as the ancient Hebrews, which allows both to ontologize themselves as full-fledged humans and the Otherites as subhuman or nonhuman. But the arbitrary nature of this model would become apparent were any of the Chosen People to usurp the God concept in order to justify violence against another tribe of seemingly Chosen People.

According to writers of African descent, Hitler, who makes use of the Bible's epistemological/ontological recursive loop, should provide the West with the example it needs to illustrate the dangers, absurdity, and injustice of constructing a political system that is based on a theological model of knowledge. I detailed the theological basis of Hitler's colonizing and genocidal project in my discussion of Wright's *The Outsider*. As the fascist character, whose philosophy is similar to Hitler's, claims: "God made him [Angelo Herndon] and his kind [Anglo-Saxons] to rule over the lower breeds" (264). Césaire takes this same view of the German dictator, for he links Hitlerism and the "very Christian bourgeois of the twentieth century." Before Europeans were the victims of Nazism, Césaire claims, "they were its accomplices." In fact, Europeans "tolerated that Nazism before it was inflicted on them, . . . they absolved it, shut their eyes to it, legitimized it, because, until then, it had been applied only to non-European peoples." Hurston is in this same interpretive tradition. By subtly linking the ancient Hebrews' treatment of the Canaanites to Hitler's Christian atrocities against fellow Europeans, Hurston found a way to expose the deepest psychological structures that have made the brutal exploitation of people of African descent a normal, everyday occurrence. Hurston gives her reader a concrete example from the Bible to clarify the nature of the then-contemporary political system.

As Hurston observes, people in the West have been shedding tears "over the fate of Holland, Belgium, France, and England," countries that have suffered at the hands of the Nazis. Hurston, however, confesses that she is not too terribly moved by these recent developments, since no one seemed to hear "a word against Holland [for] collecting one twelfth of poor people's wages in Asia" (251). Like Césaire, Hurston concludes that Hitler's crime is not really colonization or even murder; after all, European powers have been doing such things for centuries in Africa and Asia. "Hitler's crime," she claims, "is that he is actually doing a thing like that to his own kind" (251). Now we are in a position to understand why Hurston started this whole section with a description of the ancient Hebrews' domination of the Canaanites. By controlling the God concept, the ancient Hebrews have been able to define themselves as full-fledged humans and the Canaanites as "lower breeds," "no-count rascals." This theological doctrine, once internalized, makes the interests, needs, and desires of 'inferior' races, like the Canaanites, invisible; most people do not worry themselves about the rights of animals, and since Canaanites have been defined as subhuman, they are not worth worrying about. Christians, like Hitler, have usurped the Chosen People doctrine in order to justify treating Asians and Africans as the ancient Hebrews treated the Canaanites. But the moment Hitler uses that same theological doctrine to define fellow Europeans as subhuman, he is violating the tacit law of the European land—that Europeans, as Christians and therefore Chosen People, are full-fledged humans. But if Europeans can be indignant about what Hitler has done to them, so too can Canaanites, Asians, Africans, and Jews respond with equal indignation. Such is the logic implicit in the works of Hurston, Baldwin, and Wright. All three would agree that there is something fundamentally flawed with the whole model of knowledge on which western political systems have been based, and they all trace that flaw back to the God concept. This is not to say that they consider the God concept essentially evil. Rather, they consider it an empty signifier that can so easily support the political agenda of those in power and that can be used to construct certain groups of people as subhuman or nonhuman.

Not surprisingly, Hurston, like Wright, explicitly compares the political situation in Nazi Germany and the United States. In the same paragraph that deals with Hitler, she mentions how "President Roosevelt could extend his four freedoms to some people right here in America before he takes it abroad," but then she notes that what divides Germany from the United States is not political policy but the Atlantic Ocean: "Take away the ocean and he [Roosevelt] simmers down" (251). Roosevelt can fault Hitler and Germany, but he really has no leg to stand on when confronting Hitler's racist policies and practices, because the United States has in place the same kind of racist policies and practices as Germany. To quote Aimé Césaire: "When I turn on my radio, when I hear that Negroes have been lynched in America, I say that we have been lied to: Hitler is not dead" (qtd. in Fanon, *Black* 90). And what makes the United States able to justify divesting culturally designated inferiors, like African Americans, of their dignity and freedom is the God concept. As Hurston puts this in her rendition of the Old Testament, "The Lord wanted His children to have a country full of big grapes and tall corn." The egregious error of mentioning corn in a passage that is supposedly paraphrasing the Old Testament is too flagrant to ignore. A distinctively North and South American product, corn is never mentioned in the Bible. As a careful reader of the Bible, Hurston certainly would not have made such a careless mistake. So what is the purpose of including this reference in her updated version of the Bible? One logical and compelling possibility would be that Hurston is drawing our attention to the way the Chosen People mentality continues to determine the political system in America. Just as the ancient Hebrews were favored by God and given choice land, so are white Americans; and just as the Canaanites were "no-count rascals" who did not qualify as people in the strict sense of the word, so too are African Americans. At the textual level, the reference to corn unifies the political section of her Touchstone narrative by highlighting the way the Chosen People mentality of the Bible determines the political situation in Nazi Germany and racist America in the 1940s.

Consistent in the Touchstone narratives is this attempt to expose how the personal and communal faith act ultimately has destructive consequences for oppressed peoples. This explains why African American atheists frequently depict religious folk as a band of gang rapists, whose personal commitment to the faith establishes the necessary sociocultural conditions for the political construction and subsequent violation of culturally designated inferiors. At this point, let me briefly examine the sociocultural dynamic that African American atheists seek to expose. Hughes, Hurston, and Wright focus on the role the God concept plays within the black community, specifically how the relationships to family members were "shamelessly exploited" (Wright, *Black Boy* 154) to coerce erring infidels into accepting Christ. For the Christian "tribe" to accentuate the apostate's sense of guilt, it suggests that rejection of the faith does not just alienate the unbeliever from his or her family and community; it actually could destroy the family and the community. Such a situation places the infidel in the position of the "moral monster," as Wright claims, which is why both Wright and Hughes pretend to accept the faith.

And yet, in their seeming acceptance of the faith, they feel that they are ultimately contributing to the degradation and subsequent violation of their own families and communities. This is the case because the personal and communal faith act work in tandem with the ideological needs and desires of the dominant political power. Let me briefly turn to a powerful scene from Alice Walker's *The Color Purple* to illustrate what African American atheists ultimately tried to accomplish in their Touchstone narratives. In the novel, Corrine and her husband, Samuel, are missionaries who spend the major portion of their lives bringing Christ to Africa and Africans. After Corrine dies, Samuel marries Nettie, the sister of the main character. With some time to reflect on his work on the "dark continent," Samuel draws some bitter and painful conclusions. His labor in Africa, rather than being ennobling and empowering, may actually have debilitated and even destroyed Africans. To communicate this view of his experience, Samuel tells Nettie a story about Corrine's Aunt Theodosia, who was also a missionary. During an at-home, "Aunt Theodosia was going on about her African adventures, leading up to the time King Leopold II of Belgium presented her with a medal" (236). For Aunt Theodosia, this medal "validated her service as an exemplary missionary in the King's colony," so she beams with pride when telling her tale. But present at the at-home is a Harvard scholar by the name of DuBoyce, a character who is clearly based on W.E.B. DuBois. With an extremely sophisticated understanding of ideology, African history, and world politics, DuBoyce dashes Aunt Theodosia's sense of accomplishment by telling her how her missionary activity enabled Leopold to enact his brutal colonizing project in the Congo: "Rather than cherish that medal, Madame, you should regard it as a symbol of your unwitting complicity with this despot who worked to death and brutalized and eventually exterminated thousands and thousands of African peoples" (237).

In *The World and Africa*, DuBois details the seductive psychology of Christianity that so brilliantly convinced people of African descent, like Aunt Theodosia and Samuel, to contribute to their own people's degradation and violation. As DuBois claims, when he was a young boy, he was seduced by Henry Stanley's vision of Africa, specifically of the Congo, which consisted "of the great new Christian Kingdom of Congo which civilization was about to rear in the Dark Continent, to lead the natives to God" (317). Predicated on love and justice, the missionary's Christian vision could only be considered righteous, so it should come as no surprise that "Millions of pounds and dollars went into the 'conversion of the heathen' to Christianity and the education of the natives" (33). It was this surface doctrine of love and justice, which Christianity supposedly incarnates, that led everyday Europeans to believe that "the triumph of Europe [in Africa] was to the glory of God and the untrammeled power of the only people on earth who deserved to rule" (33). And yet it was exactly this kind of thinking that created the necessary sociocultural conditions for exterminating Congo brutes, to rephrase Joseph Conrad's Kurtz, or to lead so many Africans to despair, like Chinua Achebe's Okonkwo in *Things Fall Apart*.[2] Indeed, as Adam Hochschild notes in his excellent study of Leopold II, the Belgian king considered his Catholic missionaries to be as valuable as his soldiers: "Leopold subsidized the Catholics lavishly and sometimes used this financial power to deploy priests, almost as if they were soldiers, to areas where he wanted to strengthen his influence" (138). For Leopold, Christianity was the best weapon he had at his disposal, not just to garner support from fellow Europeans for his pet project in Africa but also to justify his brutal treatment of Africans. As Leopold says in his famous "Letter from the King of the Belgians," the Africans' "Primitive nature will not resist indefinitely the pressing appeals of Christian culture," and when the faith finally triumphs, Belgium will have introduced "into the vast region of the Congo all the blessings of Christian civilisation" (107–8). As a missionary, therefore, Aunt Theodosia contributed, whether she knew it or not, whether she desired to do so or not (an "unwitting complicity"), to the European domination and exploitation of Africa and Africans, and since Samuel tells this story to Nettie to indicate how he feels about his own missionary activity, we as readers can infer that he is beginning to realize how he, as a missionary, has made a similar contribution.

Put bluntly, Aunt Theodosia and Samuel's religious faith and missionary zeal are exactly what the white community needed and desired to execute its project of dominating, exploiting, and violating Africa and Africans. It is such a discovery of the way religious belief serves the political and ideological agenda of those in power that compelled so many writers, like Larsen, Wright, Hughes, and Hurston, to treat the conversion narrative as a communal act of violation. In nineteenth-century conversion narratives, the newfound belief transforms the believers' "agonized existences into ones with possibility" (9), as Yolanda Pierce has convincingly argued. But by the twentieth century, with a more complicated understanding of ideology and a new theory of "knowledge" as human constructed, many African American atheists began to cast a cynical eye on the conversion narrative.

Indeed, exposing how the local faith act serves the oppressive political and ideological agenda of those who control the intellectual means of production is the central objective in the Touchstone narratives. But here we must make a crucial distinction. These writers are not so much concerned with the specific content of the dominant religion. After all, religion and God are, as Redding, Hughes, and Hurston note, empty signifiers, so the religious content and its victims will change in relation to the dominant groups' ideological needs and desires. What concerns black atheists is personal and political agency, the capacity to create and define themselves and their world. Significantly, when DuBoyce tells Aunt Theodosia about her "unwitting complicity" with Leopold II, the first thing he mentions is Belgium's policy of "cut[ting] the hands off workers who, in the opinion of his plantation overseers, did not" work as hard as they should have (237). Amputating hands is the best way to divest Africans of personal agency and political control, and as a Christian missionary in Africa, Aunt Theodosia has played a crucial role in divesting Africans of personal and political agency over their own lives and communities, as Walker's novel suggests.

Within the context of the Touchstone narratives, it is this link between the microcommunal faith act and the macrocultural political situation that compels African American atheists to reject the God concept and to be so critical of the religious mentality. Instead of recognizing that they will achieve personal and communal agency only when they become creators and definers of "knowledge," "laws," and the "political," believers, according to African American atheists, accept their culture's "truth" as God-created truth. Such a situation places believers in a passive position with regard to their political situation. Because the faith act authorizes and legitimizes the existence of a pregiven truth, believers assume a passive position with regard to knowledge, not realizing that those truths "man himself has wrought," as Redding claims. And as Hughes consistently notes in his fiction, in believing in God and His truths, believers are actually at the epistemic mercy of those who politically control the intellectual means of production. Blacks and Jews are subject to German and American political leaders (chapter 2); blacks and women are subject to whites and men (chapter 3); the black community is subject to the white community's God/law (chapter 4); and the nonwhite world is subject to white Americans and Europeans (this chapter). In sum, what African American atheists want their readers to know and understand is this: God and his laws are, as Hurston claims, creatures of the human mind, and since humans are governed by the "selfish hand," the god and laws that humans create will reflect their selfish interests, needs, and desires. Therefore, instead of allowing themselves to be ruled by some God or some pregiven law of being, Hurston, Wright, Hughes, and Redding implicitly and explicitly urge the black community to recognize that God is a human creation and therefore to take control of their lives either by creating God and God-truths or by abolishing God altogether.

"It was a great load off my mind to say with conviction, 'God is a myth.'"

James Forman, "God Is Dead"

For the atheists in this study, the God concept is the primary political, legal, and psychological source of all our cultural woes, and this is the case because something intrinsic to theological "thinking" makes religious people incapable of self-critical reflection and unable to see unbelievers truly as people. But let me be clear about what constitutes theological thinking. As DuBois claims: "The church does not usually profess to be a group of ordinary human beings. It claims Divine Sanction. It professes to talk with God and to receive directly

His Commandments. Its ministers and members do not apparently have to acquire truth by bitter experience and long, intensive study: truth is miraculously revealed to them" (Du Bois, "Color Line" 170). Theological thinking holds that truth is a divinely sanctioned spiritual reality accessible only to God's holy elect, his Chosen People. As I have argued in chapters 1 and 2, for believers, knowing God and His truths makes a person a full-fledged human, while the lack of such Knowledge means that a person has failed to actualize his or her "highest humanity." On the basis of their knowledge of the one faith, the only truth, and the true God, believers can distinguish perverted versions of the faith from pure spirituality. Of course, believers will argue, people can commit atrocities in the name of God, but those who do so are not true believers; either they are hypocrites or they have a false understanding of the faith. The true God or the true faith, their argument goes, would never sanction oppression or injustice. From this perspective, Christians can critique specific interpretations or interpreters of Christ's claim that he is the way and the truth and the life and his claim that the only way to the Father is through him, but they could never critique Christ or true religion. In short, perverted interpretations of Christ could lead to oppression and injustice, but Christ's teachings could never be the source of injustice or oppression, so believers can never critically examine Christ or his teachings as the basis of the culture's unjust political systems.

The atheists in this study reject theological "thinking." All "knowledge" is human constructed ("our own conceptions of what things are"), so it will reflect the biases and limitations of its producers ("it is," as Hurston claims, "foolish to expect any justice untwisted by the selfish hand"). All "knowledge," therefore, is subject to critique and change. No concept or idea is inviolable, exempt from being the potential political source of injustice or oppression. Given this view, if a person says, "I believe in God, but the God that I accept is admittedly a creature of my own mind," then this person could be a believer who does not engage in theological thinking. Since such believers acknowledge that "God" is their own conception of what things are, they should be in the position to acknowledge that their psychosemiotic construction reflects their own cultural biases and limitations. In other words, by acknowledging that God is their own psychosemiotic construction, such believers would be able to engage in self-critical reflection and thereby overcome the dangers of theological thinking.

But more than that, rejecting theological thinking would enable the culture to overcome the Chosen People mentality, a mentality that effectively leads to the stratification of humanness and thereby reduces so many people to subhumans or nonhumans. This, more than anything else, is the source of the African American atheists' (as well as many other atheists') critique of faith. Because believers miraculously know God and His truths, they are in an ontological and epistemological position to determine full-fledged humanness and the political and cultural laws of being. Since those who do not subscribe to the dominant religious position are epistemological and therefore ontological inferiors, the believers need not take the infidels' views seriously. Indeed, given the believers' ability to see spiritual truth, which is the only universally valid and objectively grounded reality, they do not even acknowledge the existence of the infidel. In other words, theology's Chosen People mentality converts the nonchosen into invisible men and women (Ellison), inferior beings who must be ruled and governed (Fanon and Wright) and who must always be defined instead of definers (Morrison). It is this distinction between the spiritual (that which truly exists) and the nonspiritual (that which is ephemeral and therefore does not exist in the strict sense of the word) that has made so many in the West incapable of recognizing that their abuse, neglect, and oppression of culturally designated inferiors have been crimes against humanity (Hughes and Hurston). This is the case because the nonchosen are only temporal and spatial beings, subject to the laws of decay and death, while Chosen People are atemporal and aspatial beings, in contact with God's universal and eternal laws of being (Larsen and Hughes). In the twentieth century, with the emergence of a totalitarian political leader like Hitler who used the God concept to violate and dehumanize seemingly Chosen People, the God concept has been effectively exposed as an arbitrary idea, a semiotic vacuity that really has only one major political purpose: to perpetuate the wicked idea of human inferiority (Redding). And for the atheists in this book, it is in the Touchstone narrative that they can best expose the dangerous sociocultural dynamics of an empty concept like God. This explains why James Forman feels so liberated when he finally acknowledges that "God is a myth." Atheism makes possible personal and political freedom. And for African American atheists, the objective of the Touchstone narrative is to make a comprehensive experience of personal and political liberation a reality.

Conclusion

Black Liberation Antitheology

An Atheist Manifesto

"I would emphasize the relation of man to man rather than the relation of man to God. I would substitute the authority of Christ's insight for the authority of all ecclesiastical dogma. I would blazon across the earth: 'Love ye one another.'"

J. Saunders Redding, *On Being Negro in America*

In *On Being Negro in America*, Redding identifies the central problem with the God concept, according to African American atheists: "God is a complex composed of simple elements—mediator, father, judge, jury, executioner, and also love, virtue, charity—each of which generates a very motley collection of often contradictory ideas" (138). In short, God can be whatever the dominant culture needs it to be. God could be a figure that supports a political view in which slaves must be obedient to their masters, or it could be a figure that rejects slavery; it could be a concept that sanctions genocide, or it could be a concept that denounces violence; it could be an idea that ensures that women never serve as teachers or have authority over a man, or it could be an idea that supports gender equality; it could be the basis of keeping the races separate and pure, or it could be the reason for uniting and mixing the races. In short, the God concept is simultaneously nothing and everything; it is an idea that ultimately sanctions an "anything goes" philosophy. Since African Americans were more often than not the victims instead of the beneficiaries of the God-concept, it should come as no surprise that they produced some of the most insightful work on the deadly and destructive sociopolitical functions of theological thought.

Understanding the various sociocultural functions of the God concept, specifically as the African American atheists in this study define them, is extremely valuable for a number of reasons. First, the African American atheists' critique of the God concept provides us with a new lens for interpreting the atheistic orientation of a variety of earlier atheistic works. Rather than seeing an atheistic society as devoid of purpose and meaning, African American atheists consider a religious culture a reason for melancholic mourning. Such a view is part of a well-established atheist tradition. For instance, according to Nietzsche, it is only "in denying God" that our culture could "redeem the world" (*Twilight* 65). This is the case because theological "thinking" and the political system that it generates have, as the atheist Joseph Conrad claims, created the necessary sociopolitical conditions for the possibility of large-scale crimes, like colonization and even genocide, against culturally designated inferiors.[1] For an atheist like Virginia Woolf, that same theological "thinking" has been the basis and foundation of a political system that deprives women of personal and political agency, interpellates the poor so that they valorize their own condition of poverty, and justifies colonization.[2] In his novels *A Passage to India*, *Maurice*, and *Howards End*, the atheist E. M. Forster explains the way the God concept has been used to justify calling homosexuals subhuman beings and to ground a political caste system. For D. H. Lawrence, the God concept prohibits humans and cultures from realizing their potential for endless self-creation.[3] In short, for the atheists who honor and respect the rights and dignity of all people, it is the God concept that has made life unbearable and empty. To redeem the world, therefore, to make life more meaningful, atheism is a political and cultural must. Such is the view of the African American atheists in this book.

Second, understanding the African American atheist's critique of the God concept effectively challenges the common view that "black people are a religious people" (National Committee of Black Churchmen, qtd. in Jones 38) or that "Religion in some form or other appears to be an Africanism" (J. Deotis Roberts, qtd. in Jones 38). At this point, I want to take issue with a scholar for whom I have immense respect and admiration. In his provocative essay "Religious Humanism: Its Problems and Prospects in Black Religion and Culture," William R. Jones argues that black humanism and nontheism must be given equal consideration in the histories of African American religion. This is the case, Jones argues, because blacks have made significant contributions to our ever-evolving understanding of humanism and have produced some insightful critiques of religion and the God concept. Understanding black humanism and nontheism, therefore, would further the cause of "radical freedom/autonomy as the essence of human reality" (34). While I certainly agree with Jones that the black "nontheistic perspective" (27) is extremely valuable and therefore needs to be given more scholarly attention, I am less convinced that it should be recognized as a religion or in a religious sense.

For Jones, the major reason why black humanism and nontheism have been marginalized is because "nontheism, by definition, is excluded as a religious perspective" (37). Were the intellectual community to recognize nontheism and humanism as religions, both would get more scholarly attention and cultural legitimacy. At this juncture, Jones's argument becomes suspect. So that African American humanism and nontheism are taken more seriously, we should label them religions. Certainly, this argument does not establish the fact that humanism and nontheism are religions; it just demands that we treat the two as such for a pragmatic purpose, to get them more scholarly attention.

What is really behind Jones's argument, however, is his assumption that people of African descent are religious. After quoting a couple of passages about blacks being innately religious, that is, religious in a theistic sense, Jones claims: "Several points here merit comment. Unless religion and theism are equated, these statements are meaningless. Moreover, it should also be noted that here theism is not simply advanced as the majority viewpoint but rather as the normative perspective and the yardstick by which one identifies the authentic black consciousness. Indeed, by defining black religion exclusively in theistic terms and thus failing to make an allowance for nontheistic perspectives, these statements come close to making the acceptance of theism a defining characteristic of being black" (38). Because there are plenty of blacks who do not believe in God, Jones, as a black humanist, rejects "the arrogant assumption that the black religious experience is somehow exhausted by the theistic experience" (40). For Jones, by broadening the idea of "black religion," it would be possible to call nontheism and humanism religions. But more than that, he would be able to claim that being religious, though not necessarily a believer in God, is "a defining characteristic of being black." While Jones questions and challenges the assumption that blacks are religious in a theistic sense, he never questions or challenges the view that black people are, by nature, religious.

Given the arguments of the African American atheists in this book, however, Jones's primary assumption needs significant qualification. What distinguishes the atheist from the theist, at least according to the atheists in this book, is their orientation toward knowledge. Theists assume the existence of a mind-independent Truth that they are best epistemologically stationed to know, whereas atheists claim that "knowledge" is a necessary psychosemiotic construction that assumes a provisional form in and through a semiotic sign. For atheists, when humans construct a discourse about mind-independent objects, they must acknowledge that their discourse is, to some degree, their own conception of what things are. Such a view does not mean that language, concepts, and knowledge are always false and useless. It just means that there is nothing that makes any particular discourse objectively true or universally valid. As Damon suggests, for a community to work, we need to build bridges between each other through the promise of the social contract, but Damon would be the first to acknowledge that the promise is a human-constructed idea that should be subjected to a never-ending process of interrogation, deconstruction, and a subsequent reconstruction. Does this mean that blacks are essentially nonreligious beings? For Damon, we could construct a particular community as religious, but if that discourse does not succeed, then we could and should construct it in a nonreligious way.

In direct contradiction of Jones and the traditional view that black people are essentially religious, Redding claims: "I simply rejected religion. I rejected God" (144). And yet, to conclude *On Being Negro in America*, Redding suggests that "Christianity promises a cure for our American sickness" (155) of racism. This is not a contradiction, though it seems to be. For Redding, Christ was not God, because there is no God, but as a person, he was not such a bad guy. In fact, Redding considers the "practicality" of Christ's "injunctions" (149) to be noble. For Redding, it would be possible to save Christ and even Christianity if the culture were to secularize both by disposing of the God concept and theological thinking: "But it [Christianity] must be made truly a way of life in which the dignity and brotherhood of man is the first principle. Perhaps it should be divorced from mysticism and otherworldliness—from theology. I would emphasize the relation of man to man rather than the relation of man to God" (156). As an atheist, Redding considers "knowledge" psychosemiotic construction, which means that claims like Christ is God or blacks are essentially religious would be human-constructed ideas instead of metaphysical Truths. As Redding observes, "[R]ace is a myth: it is artificial" (152). Or, to put this in the words of Baldwin, "Color is not a human or a personal reality; it is a political reality" (104). According to this view, it is possible to construct a race as religious, but it is important to realize that such constructions are a myth, an artificial construction of the larger language community. Therefore, it would be incoherent to suggest, as does Jones, that being religious "is a defining characteristic of being black."

For Redding, therefore, religion could be politically effective and life affirming were it to bring about a "far-going social transformation and evolution" (146). So Redding, like all the African American atheists in this study, does not suggest abolishing religion. What he does suggest is that we recognize that God is a human-construct ("the qualities attributed to God represent man's acknowledged needs" [146]), a "being" that should evolve in relation to the needs of the community. According to this view, for "god" to become an empowering concept for all people, the human community must acknowledge that it is a human-construction that evolves in relation to the culture's ever-shifting and ever-evolving needs, and all people must be able to participate in "god's" construction. Only when everyone acknowledges that "god" takes his or her cue from humans can religion become a life-affirming experience. But Redding suggests that religion should only play a role within the culture if it contributes to the one thing necessary: "far-going social transformation." If religion does not enable people to construct themselves as empowered agents, then the people must construct themselves outside and beyond the confines of religion.

At this point, let me briefly summarize the major reasons why African American atheists would ultimately reject the view that blacks are by nature religious. First but not foremost, Redding is a perfect counterexample, for he is an African American who blatantly and unequivocally rejects God and religion. To maintain the view that people of African descent are essentially religious, religious folk would have to do one of two things. They would have to claim that Redding is an aberration, a freak of nature, someone who lays claim to an African heritage but who lacks one of the defining characteristics of being black. Consequently, his rejection of religion does not undermine the claim that people of African descent are essentially religious. Or they would have to claim that they have privileged knowledge which Redding lacks. According to this view, Redding, whether he knows it or not, is religious. The problem is that he just does not understand the true definition of religion, and therefore he does not really understand himself. To be sure, the religious folk who use this argument conceive of knowledge as discovery (I examine this religious mentality in chapters 1 and 2), and if Redding refuses to accept their definition, then he is either intellectually inferior or simply intractable.

The next reason why the atheists in this study would reject the claim that blacks are essentially religious is because they denounce the epistemological arrogance and rhetorical imperialism that make such a claim possible. Both the concepts of race and God are human constructions, so the culture could decide to construct "blacks" as "religious," but such an idea is just a concept that assumes a provisional form within a particular cultural and discursive context. If, however, the culturally constructed idea of blacks as religious ceases to create the conditions for positive social transformation, then we could, as a culture, agree to construct blacks or any other race as nonreligious. Because there is no mind-independent concept dangling from some heaven of ideas, knowledge is, at least for the atheists in this study, a human construction, which means that it is incoherent to say that blacks are inherently religious.

The final reason why understanding the African American atheists' critique of the sociocultural dynamics of faith is extremely valuable relates to the current resurgence in religion. A casual survey of recent political events indicates that the God concept and theological "thinking" are very much alive. From Mohammed Atta's faith-based initiative of flying jets into buildings with innocent people aboard, to President Bush's reintroduction of the word *evil* into the public discourse, to Pope John Paul II's shockingly insensitive and inhumane decision to declare homosexuality a part of an "ideology of evil," there has been a profound rejection of knowledge as democratic construction and a return to knowledge as inviolable truth. In short, knowledge is becoming theological again and with a vengeance. Consequently, there have been and will continue to be more victims of faith, and the African American atheists in this study provide a comprehensive view of the strategies that believers will use to violate their culturally designated inferiors with impunity.

If the African American atheists in this study enable us to see the sophisticated strategies of abuse that believers are likely to deploy, they also provide a way of avoiding those same crimes against culturally designated inferiors. Instead of using the God concept to justify dubbing some people as superior and others as inferiors; instead of using it to divest certain disempowered groups of basic human rights; instead of using it to vindicate intrusive and inhumane political policies, the atheists in this study endorse a democratic construction of "God," a political system that would allow all "humans" to take control of their humanity and to construct themselves as empowered agents. Such a goal will only be achieved, as the writers in this study suggest, when we finally acknowledge that God is a creature of our own minds and that the God concept should have only one purpose: positive social transformation. To quote Baldwin: "If the concept of God has any validity or any use, it can only be to make us larger, freer, and more loving. If God cannot do this, then it is time we got rid of Him" (47).

Given the social transformation and communal empowerment objectives of the atheists in this study, we could dub their writings a liberation atheism or a liberation antitheology. In order to bring into sharp focus the distinctive nature of their view, I want to imagine how the African American atheists in this book would respond to the work of two first-rate contemporary black theologians, Albert J. Raboteau and James H. Cone. For Raboteau, the black appropriation of the scriptures functioned to empower and to liberate African Americans, because blacks were able to offer an interpretation that contradicted the white supremacist approach. For example, when discussing how African Americans identified with the ancient Hebrews of Exodus, Raboteau claims that the biblical story "contradicted the claim made by defenders of slavery that God intended Africans to be slaves" and therefore "Exodus proved that slavery was against God's will and that slavery would end someday" (44). But as Hurston observes, the ancient Hebrews, who, like white westerners, had the military might to control the intellectual means of production, were able to ontologize themselves as the Chosen People. Of course, the Canaanites, like African Americans, could have claimed that they were the Chosen People as well, but given their lack of political power, it would not have mattered, since the ancient Hebrews had the political power to ontologize the Canaanites as "no-count rascals," just as white westerners had the political power to ontologize blacks as "lower breeds." So within their own communities, the Canaanites and African Americans could have appropriated the Chosen People title and mentality. But at a sociopolitical level, this would have done little or nothing to alter their condition in the national political arena. After all, even though the ancient Hebrews were set free in Exodus, thus seemingly justifying the abolition of slavery, this did not stop God or the ancient Hebrews from enslaving many others in Leviticus, Deuteronomy, and so many other books of the Bible, and if the white communities were the ones with the political power to enact the Chosen People mentality at the sociocultural level, it would not matter very much if the Canaanites or African Americans considered themselves Chosen People. Therefore, Hurston would argue, the God concept and the Chosen People mentality may have provided hope and inspired oppressed people to take control of their own lives, but it also inspired the oppressors and justified their construction, domination, exploitation, and ultimate violation of culturally designated inferiors at the political, psychological, and emotional levels.

In his justly famous study, *A Black Theology of Liberation*, Cone addresses the possibility of abandoning "God-language." Cone realizes that the God concept is extremely powerful and effective in the project of liberating the oppressed, but he is also acutely aware of its function "as an instrument to further the cause of human humiliation" (107). As he notes, in white supremacist America, "blacks were enslaved and Indians exterminated—in the name of God and freedom" (109). But the God that whites have created "is an idol, created by the racist bastards" (114), and as such, it bears no resemblance to the God of "the authentic prophetic tradition" (109), which is the "God of the oppressed," that is, "a God of revolution who breaks the chains of slavery" (112). Therefore, Cone argues that "black people must perform the iconoclastic task of smashing false images" (114), which means demolishing the white supremacist God. In destroying the white God, Cone does not want blacks to abandon God altogether, for he believes that there is a "religious dimension inherent in the black community." Indeed, the "black community," Cone claims, is "a religious community, a community that views its liberation as the work of the divine" (112).

For someone like Wright, Cone's approach to both God and knowledge contributes to rather than solves the problem plaguing western culture. Wright would agree with Cone that western culture has used the God concept and theological thinking to justify horrible crimes, and he would also agree that we need to expose and demolish the conceptual apparatuses that have made such violations a regular occurrence, but he would reject Cone's appeal to an "authentic prophetic tradition" and his claim that there is a "religious dimension inherent in the black community." For Redding and Wright, the primary problem with western culture is not simply its racist content, bad as that has been; the problem is its implicit claim to authentic knowledge, a claim that has enabled white westerners to justify dubbing themselves full-fledged humans and nonwhites and nonwesterners subhuman or nonhuman. When Cone decides to speak in the same way that theists in the West have spoken for centuries, he ends up becoming what he tries to defeat ("[I]f you," Cross Damon observes, "fought men who tried to conquer you in terms of total power you too had to use total power and in the end you became what you tried to defeat."). The disease of theological thinking "has reached out and claimed" Cone, too. To escape this cycle of destruction, Wright would not necessarily claim that Cone should abandon God or religion. According to Wright, Cone could not claim that he has epistemological access to an authentic religious tradition or the black community's nature. For African American atheists, the most that Cone can legitimately claim is that he belongs to a specific religious tradition that he and his community have created. But, as the atheists in this study suggest, by stressing that God and religion are nothing more than his and his community's own conceptions of what things are, Cone would avoid the primary pitfall of the religious epistemology, which is the implicit claim to full-fledged humanness (Chosen Person) on the basis of a person's capacity to have authentic Knowledge or Knowledge of a person's or a people's nature. In short, according to the liberation atheists in this study, Cone would create the conditions for personal autonomy and communal agency not by adopting the West's oppressive system of authentic, God-created knowledge but by abandoning the idea of a God independent of the human mind altogether. Were the world community to do such a thing, no one would be able to claim that they were in possession of an authentic religion or a true God, because everyone would have to admit, in all humility, that God is nothing more than a creature of our own minds and that religion is our own conception of what things are.

To conclude, we could say that, while the atheists in this study ultimately do not endorse abolishing the God concept or religion, they do suggest that there is ample evidence that the God concept cannot bring about positive social transformation for all people. So maybe it is time to give a thoroughgoing atheist politics a chance. Maybe then we will finally realize the dream of a pluralist democracy that is committed to the project of empowering all people instead of just a chosen few.

Notes

Introduction

1. There are certainly many white atheists who did not consider God's death an occasion for despair. Such rejoicing atheists include Friedrich Nietzsche, Virginia Woolf, and Michel Foucault. For a discussion of the differences between despairing and rejoicing atheists, see my essay, "Atheism and Sadism: Nietzsche and Woolf on Post-God Discourse."

2. In his introduction to the *Dynamics of Faith*, Tillich claims that a misunderstanding of faith "confuses, misleads, creates alternately skepticism and fanaticism, rejection of genuine religion and subjection to substitutes." As I will argue throughout this book, the idea of a true concept of faith or a genuine religion is based on a misunderstanding of the construction of knowledge and the evolution of ideas.

3. For examples of the postcolonial critique of the God concept, see my essays "The Moral Conditions for Genocide in Joseph Conrad's *Heart of Darkness*" and "Frantz Fanon on the Theology of Colonization."

4. I take this passage from an unpublished lecture that Forster delivered in 1909. I am currently editing and annotating this lecture, which will appear in a forthcoming issue of *Journal of Modern Literature*.

5. For a more in-depth analysis of this idea of being physiologically false, see my essay "Killing God, Liberating the 'Subject': Nietzsche and Post-God Freedom."

Chapter 1

1. In *Liberation Historiography*, John Ernest notes that in liberation theology circles there is a clear understanding of the function of ideology in the construction of a religious agenda: "[L]iberation theology asserts that institutionally sanctioned religious thought is never politically neutral but rather always functions within a certain sociopolitical theater, and accordingly must always function in a dynamic and contingent relation to the dominant economic and political forces that shape the lives of the people" (15).

2. For excellent studies of atheists within this tradition, see James Thrower's *Western Atheism: A Short History*, Kai Nielsen's *Naturalism and Religion*, and David Berman's *A History of Atheism in Britain: From Hobbes to Russell*.

3. In *The System of Nature*, Baron d'Holbach offered a strictly secular account of the world. According to Berman, d'Holbach was the first speculative atheist in the western intellectual tradition, which means that he was the first to develop a coherent system that takes an atheistic view of the world as its point of departure.

In *The Essence of Christianity*, Feuerbach treated the God concept as psychological projection.

For Darwin, given the ruthless way that the ichneumon wasp devours its prey, it was impossible to believe that a benevolent deity had created or governs the universe. For an insightful analysis of Darwin's inability to believe, see Stephen Jay Gould's essay "Nonmoral Nature."

In the late nineteenth century, Leslie Stephen brilliantly formulated a humanistic-based agnostic philosophy. See Stephen, *An Agnostic's Apology: Poisonous Opinions, in Selected Writings in British Intellectual History*.

Friedrich Nietzsche launched one of the most vicious and compelling attacks on belief. For some of his most pointed remarks about the value of atheism and the necessity of skepticism, see *Anti-Christ, The Gay Science, On the Genealogy of Morals,* and *Twilight of the Idols*.

Bertrand Russell based his epistemological skepticism on a rigorous epistemology and historical analyses. For excellent essays that clarify his skepticism, see *Why I Am Not a Christian*.

For one of the most brilliant essays to justify an atheistic worldview, see Antony Flew, "The Presumption of Atheism."

4. For an excellent example of the genealogical analysis of theology and the God concept, see Nietzsche, *On the Genealogy of Morals*.

5. In *A History of Atheism in Britain*, David Berman sums up the view of the epistemological skeptic: "God is being defied because it is unethical to believe in Him. A God who wants us to believe in Him in clear opposition to the available evidence is simply immoral and incredible" (246).

6. It was not until the nineteenth century that scholars could actually suggest that theology leads—necessarily—to extreme forms of physical and psychological violence. Of the works that theorize the brutality inherent in faith, Feuerbach's *Essence of Christianity* was certainly the most important. Only eight years after the publication of this work, James A. Froude published *The Nemesis of Faith*, a book that also examines the violence and intolerance at the core of religious belief. But it would not be until the twentieth century that the most incisive critiques of the psychology of belief would occur.

7. Regina M. Schwartz has published a very insightful book, *The Curse of Cain: The Violent Legacy of Monotheism*, in which she tries to detail why believers so often perpetrate extreme acts of violence against other people. Schwartz focuses on the monotheistic principles of exclusion and scarcity, exposing how belief in a single God leads to a particularly violent construction of a communal identity.

8. In *Black Skin, White Masks*, Fanon mentions how the Bible functions to instantiate the master/slave relation: "All forms of exploitation resemble one another. They all seek the source of their necessity in some edict of a Biblical nature" (88). This comment merely anticipates the more sophisticated analysis of the function of the God concept that we see in *The Wretched of the Earth*.

9. For a brilliant analysis of the way the British have used the theological mentality to justify colonizing African countries, see R. B. Cunninghame Graham's essay "'Bloody Niggers.'"

10. My allusion in this sentence to Franz Kafka and Paul Celan is directly relevant to the argument of this chapter. In *Black Skin, White Masks*, Fanon quotes Aimé Césaire, who claims that Hitler, as a Christian, did to Europeans what Europeans had been doing to minorities for centuries (90–91). Both Kafka and Celan lost their families during the Shoah, and Kafka's parable of the man standing before the door of the law (as well as Celan's poem "To One who stood before the Door") makes considerable sense if we interpret their experiences, as Jews, through the theology of colonization that I detail in this chapter. For a more specific example of this approach, see my essay "Poetry as Overt Critique of Theology: A Reading of Paul Celan's 'Es war Erde in Ihnen.'"

11. For a more extensive analysis of Eliot's justification for banishing free-thinking Jews, see my essay "Virginia Woolf and T. S. Eliot: An Atheist's Commentary on the Epistemology of Belief."

12. This point is made brilliantly in Toni Morrison's *Beloved*: "[D]efinitions belonged to the definers—not the defined" (190).

13. For discussions of a posttheological model of subject-production, see my essays "Killing God, Liberating the 'Subject': Nietzsche and Post-God Freedom" and "Atheism and Sadism: Nietzsche and Woolf on Post-God Discourse."

Chapter 2

1. For an excellent discussion of the various antihumanisms, see Martin Halliwell and Andy Mousley, *Critical Humanism: Humanist/Anti-Humanist Dialogues*.

2. For excellent examples of this approach to defining the human, see Immanuel Kant, *Critique of Practical Reason* and Friedrich Schiller, *On the Aesthetic Education of Man*.

3. For the justly famous treatment of this view of the human, see Arthur O. Lovejoy, *The Great Chain of Being*.

4. For discussions of this traditional view of language, see Jacques Derrida, "Force and Signification" and *Of Grammatology*, and Richard Rorty, *Contingency, Irony, and Solidarity*.

5. Henry Louis Gates Jr. notes how prominent philosophers like David Hume, Immanuel Kant, and G.W.F. Hegel take the subhuman inferiority of the African as a given.

6. Wright met Césaire in 1946 in Paris, and in 1950 the two organized the exhibit "Revelation of Negro Art." For a discussion of Wright's contact with Césaire, see Michel Fabre's *The Unfinished Quest of Richard Wright* (317–19).

7. Like Wright, Césaire criticizes humanism but ultimately proclaims himself a "humanist."

8. For a similar approach to Wright, see Fabre, "Richard Wright, French Existentialism, and *The Outsider*" (189).

9. It is worth noting that Hitler never left the Catholic Church and the Church never ex-communicated him. It is also significant that a poll taken in 1940 indicates that 95 percent of Germans considered themselves Christians. See James Carroll, *Constantine's Sword: The Church and the Jews: A History* (28, 44).

10. In *Mein Kampf,* Hitler uses the word *atheist* only twice, once referring to Jews (307) and once referring to Marxists (565).

11. For some excellent discussions of Wright's humanism, see Michel Fabre, *The Unfinished Quest of Richard Wright*, and Clyde Taylor, "Black Writing as Immanent Humanism."

12. Cross's rejection of humanism may sound similar to Heidegger's claim in "Letter on Humanism," but actually Heidegger was really a postfoundationalist humanist, as Derrida and Iain Chambers argue. See Jacques Derrida, "The Ends of Man," and Iain Chambers, *Culture after Humanism: History, Culture, Subjectivity*. I will offer a new interpretation of Heidegger's humanism at the end of this chapter.

Chapter 3

1. This translation I take from Harold Bloom's *Ruin the Sacred Truths: Poetry and Belief from the Bible to the Present* (15).

2. For excellent discussions of the traumatic experience, see Judith Lewis Herman's *Trauma and Recovery*, Suzette A. Henke's *Shattered Subjects: Trauma and Testimony in Women's Life-Writing*, and the essays in Cathy Caruth's *Trauma: Explorations in Memory.*

3. In Sieglinde Lemke's excellent book, *Primitivist Modernism: Black Culture and the Origins of Transatlantic Modernism*, jazz is defined as distinctly secular: "Jazz was profane, not sacred; it was urban, not rural. While the blues had strong ties to church songs and folk expressions, early jazz musicians played in bars and music clubs" (61).

Chapter 4

1. Arnold Rampersad has documented Hughes's deep admiration of and respect for Whitman in his *Life of Langston Hughes* (28–29).

2. For an excellent study of the Scottsboro trials, see James Goodman's *Stories of Scottsboro.*

3. In 1938, Benjamin E. Mays examined the rise of agnosticism and atheism in the African American community in *The Negro's God as Reflected in His Literature* (218–44). This antireligious and anti-God development helps explain a character like Bert.

Chapter 5

1. My theory of the Touchstone narrative stands in stark contrast to Peter A. Dorsey's discussion of the African American anticonversion narrative. The word *anticonversion* carries a negative connotation. While I agree with Dorsey that writers like Hurston and Wright resisted and ultimately rejected the conversion experience, their autobiographies do more than just renounce God and religion. Both writers spend considerable time analyzing and evaluating the God concept and religion. My coinage of the phrase *Touchstone narrative* is intended to articulate not just their critical stance but also their attempt to evaluate the quality and worth of the God concept and religion.

2. For a detailed analysis of Conrad's brilliant critique of British imperialism, see my essay "The Moral Conditions for Genocide in Joseph Conrad's *Heart of Darkness*."

Conclusion

1. See my essay "The Moral Conditions for Genocide in Joseph Conrad's *Heart of Darkness*."

2. For a discussion of Woolf's treatment of the God concept, see my essays "Virginia Woolf and T. S. Eliot: An Atheist's Commentary on the Epistemology of Belief," "Atheism and Sadism: Nietzsche and Woolf on Post-God Discourse," and "The Gender of Atheism in Virginia Woolf's 'A Simple Melody.'"

3. Lawrence examines this idea in most detail in *Women in Love*.

Works Cited

Achebe, Chinua. *Things Fall Apart*. New York: Anchor, 1994.

Allen, Norm R., Jr. *African American Humanism: An Anthology*. Buffalo, N.Y.: Prometheus, 1991.

Baldwin, James. *The Fire Next Time*. New York: Vintage Books, 1993.

Barnett, Pamela E. "'My Picture of You Is, After All, the True Helga Crane': Portraiture and Identity in Nella Larsen's *Quicksand*." *Signs: A Journal of Women in Culture and Society* 20 (Spring 1995): 575–600.

Berman, David. *A History of Atheism in Britain: From Hobbes to Russell*. New York: Routledge, 1988.

Bhabha, Homi K. *The Location of Culture*. New York: Routledge, 1994.

Bloom, Harold. *Ruin the Sacred Truths: Poetry and Belief From the Bible to the Present*. Cambridge, Mass.: Harvard University Press, 1989.

Byatt, A. S. "Morpho Eugenia." *Angels and Insects*. New York: Vintage Books, 1994. 3–183

Carby, Hazel V. *Reconstructing Womanhood: The Emergence of the Afro-American Woman Novelist*. New York: Oxford University Press, 1987.

Carroll, Charles. *The Negro a Beast*. 1900. Salem: Ayer, 1991.

Carroll, James. *Constantine's Sword: The Church and the Jews: A History*. Boston: Houghton Mifflin, 2001.

Caruth, Cathy. *Trauma: Explorations in Memory*. Baltimore: Johns Hopkins University Press, 1995.

Césaire, Aimé. *Discourse on Colonialism*. Trans. Joan Pinkham. New York: Monthly Review Press, 1972.

Chambers, Iain. *Culture After Humanism: History, Culture, Subjectivity*. London: Routledge, 2001.

Cone, James H. *A Black Theology of Liberation*. Philadelphia: J. B. Lippincott, 1970.

———. *Speaking the Truth: Ecumenism, Liberation, and Black Theology*. Maryknoll, N.Y.: Orbis, 1999.

Cornell, Drucilla. *The Philosophy of the Limit*. New York: Routledge, 1992.

Cover, Robert. "Violence and the Word." *Narrative, Violence, and the Law: The Essays of Robert Cover*. Ann Arbor: University of Michigan Press, 1995. 203–38.

Cunninghame Graham, R. B. "'Bloody Niggers.'" *Selected Writings of Cunninghame Graham*. Ed. Cedric Watts. Rutherford, N.J.: Fairleigh Dickinson University Press; London: Associated University Presses, 1981. 58–67.

Derrida, Jacques. "Force and Signification." *Writing and Difference*. Trans. Alan Bass. Chicago: University of Chicago Press, 1967. 3–30.

———. "Force of Law: The 'Mystical Foundation of Authority.'" *Deconstruction and the Possibility of Justice*. Ed. Drucilla Cornell, Michael Rosenfeld, and David Gray Carlson. New York: Routledge, 1992. 3–67.

———. *Of Grammatology*. Trans. Gayatri Chakravorty Spivak. Baltimore: Johns Hopkins University Press, 1976.

———. "The Ends of Man." *Margins of Philosophy*. Trans. Alan Bass. Chicago: University of Chicago Press, 1967. 109–36.

Donne, John. *John Donne: The Complete English Poems*. Ed. A. J. Smith. New York: Penguin, 1981.

Dorsey, Peter A. *Sacred Estrangement: The Rhetoric of Conversion in Modern American Autobiography*. University Park: Pennsylvania State University Press, 1993.

Douglass, Frederick. *Narrative of the Life of Frederick Douglass. The Classic Slave Narratives*. Ed. Henry Louis Gates Jr. New York: Penguin, 1987. 245–331.

Du Bois, W.E.B. "The Color Line and the Church." *Du Bois on Religion*. Ed. Phil Zuckerman. Walnut Creek, Calif.: AltaMira, 2000. 169–71.

———. *The World and Africa: An Inquiry into the Part Which Africa Has Played in World History*. New York: International, 1965.

Baron d'Holbach. *The System of Nature*. New York: Garland, 1984.

Eliot, T. S. *After Strange Gods: A Primer of Modern Heresy*. New York: Harcourt Brace, 1934.

———. "Religion and Literature." *Essays Ancient and Modern*. London: Faber and Faber, 1945. 92–115.

Ellison, Ralph. *Invisible Man*. New York: Vintage Books, 1995.

Equiano, Olaudah. *The Life of Gustavus Vasa. The Classic Slave Narratives*. Ed. Henry Louis Gates Jr. New York: Penguin, 1987. 1–182.

Ernest, John. *Liberation Historiography: African American Writers and the Challenge of History, 1794–1861*. Chapel Hill: University of North Carolina Press, 2004.

Fabre, Michel. "Richard Wright, French Existentialism, and *The Outsider*." *Critical Essays on Richard Wright*. Ed. Yoshinobu Hakutani. Boston: G. K. Hall, 1982. 182–98.

———. *The Unfinished Quest of Richard Wright*. Trans. Isabel Barzun. Urbana: University of Illinois Press, 1993.

Fanon, Frantz. *Black Skin, White Masks*. Trans. Charles Lam Markmann. New York: Grove, 1967.

———. *The Wretched of the Earth*. Trans. Constance Farrington. New York: Grove, 1963.

Felski, Rita. "Modernist Studies and Cultural Studies: Reflections on Method." *Modernism/Modernity* 10:3 (2003): 501–17.

Feuerbach, Ludwig. *The Essence of Christianity*. Trans. George Eliot. Buffalo, N.Y.: Prometheus, 1989.

Flew, Antony. "The Presumption of Atheism." *Contemporary Perspectives on Religious Epistemology*. Ed. R. Douglas Geivett and Brenda Sweetman. New York: Oxford University Press, 1992. 19–32.

Forman, James. "Corrupt Black Preachers" and "God Is Dead: A Question of Power." *By These Hands: A Documentary History of African American Humanism*. Ed. Anthony B. Pinn. New York: New York University Press, 2001. 261–86.

Foucault, Michel. *The Order of Things: An Archaeology of the Human Sciences*. New York: Vintage Books, 1994.

———. "A Preface to Transgression." *Language, Counter-Memory, Practice: Selected Essays and Interviews*. Eds. and trans. Donald F. Bouchard and Sherry Simon. Ithaca, N.Y.: Cornell University Press, 1977. 29–52.

Frederick, John T. *The Darkened Sky: Nineteenth-Century American Novelists and Religion*. Notre Dame, Ind.: Notre Dame University Press, 1969.

Freud, Sigmund. *Letters of Sigmund Freud*. Trans. Tania and James Stern. New York: Basic Books, 1960.

Froude, James A. *The Nemesis of Faith*. London: Libris, 1988.

Forster, E. M. *Maurice*. New York: W. W. Norton, 1993.

———. *A Passage to India*. Orlando: Harcourt, 1984.

Gates, Henry Louis, Jr. "Editor's Introduction: Writing 'Race' and the Difference It Makes." *"Race," Writing, and Difference*. Ed. Henry Louis Gates Jr. Chicago: University of Chicago Press, 1985. 1–20.

Goodman, James. *Stories of Scottsboro*. New York: Random House, 1994.

Gould, Stephen Jay. "Nonmoral Nature." *Natural History* 91:2 (1982): 19–26.

Hakutani, Yoshinobu. "Richard Wright's *The Outsider* and Albert Camus's *The Stranger*." *Richard Wright: A Collection of Critical Essays*. Ed. Arnold Rampersad. Englewood Cliffs, N.J.: Prentice Hall, 1995.

Halliwell, Martin, and Andy Mousley. *Critical Humanism: Humanist/Anti-Humanist Dialogues*. Edinburgh: Edinburgh University Press, 2003.

Heidegger, Martin. "Letter on Humanism." *Basic Writings*. San Francisco: Harper and Row, 1977. 193–242.

Henke, Suzette A. *Shattered Subjects: Trauma and Testimony in Women's Life-Writing*. New York: St. Martin's, 1998.

Herman, Judith Lewis. *Trauma and Recovery*. New York: Basic Books, 1992.

Hitler, Adolf. *Mein Kampf*. Trans. Ralph Manheim. Boston: Houghton Mifflin, 1971.

———. "Speech of February 15, 1933." *My New Order*. Ed. Raoul de Roussy de Sales. New York: Reynal and Hitchcock, 1941. 148–50.

Hochschild, Adam. *King Leopold's Ghost: A Story of Greed, Terror, and Heroism in Colonial Africa.* Boston: Houghton Mifflin, 1998

Holy Bible: The New American Bible. Nashville: Thomas Nelson, 1971.

Hughes, Langston. *The Big Sea.* New York: Hill and Wang, 1993.

————. "Christ in Alabama." *The Collected Poems of Langston Hughes.* Ed. Arnold Rampersad. New York: Vintage Books, 1995. 143.

————. "Father and Son." *The Ways of White Folks.* New York: Vintage Classics, 1990. 207–55.

————. "Gods." *The Collected Poems of Langston Hughes.* Ed. Arnold Rampersad. New York: Vintage Books, 1995. 37.

————. "Goodbye Christ." *The Collected Poems of Langston Hughes.* Ed. Arnold Rampersad. New York: Vintage Books, 1995. 166–67.

————. "Professor." *Langston Hughes: Short Stories.* Ed. Akiba Sullivan Harper. New York: Hill and Wang, 1996. 101–7.

————. "Trouble with the Angels." *Langston Hughes: Short Stories.* Ed. Akiba Sullivan Harper. New York: Hill and Wang, 1996. 120–25.

————. "The Young Glory of Him." *Langston Hughes: Short Stories.* Ed. Akiba Sullivan Harper. New York: Hill and Wang, 1996. 10–16.

Humanist Manifestos I and II. Ed. Paul Kurtz. Buffalo, N.Y.: Prometheus, 1973.

Hurston, Zora Neale. *Dust Tracks on a Road.* New York: HarperPerennial, 1991.

Iser, Wolfgang. *The Fictive and the Imaginary: Charting Literary Anthropology.* Baltimore: Johns Hopkins University Press, 1993.

Jacobs, Harriet. *Incidents in the Life of a Slave Girl. The Classic Slave Narratives.* Ed. Henry Louis Gates Jr. New York: Penguin, 1987. 333–515.

Johnson, Barbara. "The Quicksands of the Self: Nella Larsen and Heinz Kohut." *Telling Facts: History and Narration in Psychoanalysis.* Baltimore: Johns Hopkins University Press, 1992. 184–99.

Jones, William R. "Religious Humanism: Its Problems and Prospects in Black Religion and Culture." *By These Hands: A Documentary History of African American Humanism.* Ed. Anthony B. Pinn. New York: New York University Press, 2001. 25–54.

Kant, Immanuel. *Critique of Practical Reason.* Trans. Lewis White Beck. Upper Saddle River: Prentice Hall, 1993.

Kazin, Alfred. *God and the American Writer.* New York: Alfred A. Knopf, 1997.

King Leopold II. "Letter From the King of the Belgians." *Fictions of Empire.* Ed. John Kucich. Boston: Houghton Mifflin, 2003. 106–8.

Lackey, Michael. "Atheism and Sadism: Nietzsche and Woolf on Post-God Discourse." *Philosophy and Literature* 24:2 (October 2000): 346–63.

————. "Frantz Fanon on the Theology of Colonization." *Journal of Colonialism and Colonial History* 3:2 (2002): 1–29.

————. "The Gender of Atheism in Virginia Woolf's 'A Simple Melody.'" *Studies in Short Fiction* 35:1 (Winter 1998): 49–63.

———. "The Ideological Function of the God-Concept in William Faulkner's *Light in August*." *Faulkner Journal* (Fall 2005/Spring 2006): 40–62.

———. "Killing God, Liberating the 'Subject': Nietzsche and Post-God Freedom." *Journal of the History of Ideas* 60:4 (October 1999): 737–54.

———. "The Moral Conditions for Genocide in Joseph Conrad's *Heart of Darkness*." *College Literature* 32:1 (Winter 2005): 20–41.

———. "Poetry as Overt Critique of Theology: A Reading of Paul Celan's 'Es war Erde in Ihnen.'" *Monatshefte: für deutschsprachige Literatur und Kultur* 94:4 (Winter 2002): 427–40.

———. "Virginia Woolf and T. S. Eliot: An Atheist's Commentary on the Epistemology of Belief." *Woolf Studies Annual* 8 (2002): 63–91.

Lamont, Corliss. *Philosophy of Humanism*. New York: Continuum, 1990.

Larsen, Nella. *Passing. Quicksand and Passing*. New Brunswick, N.J.: Rutgers University Press, 1998. 137–242.

———. *Quicksand. Quicksand and Passing*. New Brunswick, N.J.: Rutgers University Press, 1998. 1–135.

Lawrence, D. H. *The Complete Poems of D. H. Lawrence* 2 vols. Eds. Vivian de Sola Pinto and Warren Roberts. London: Heinemann, 1964.

———. *Women in Love*. New York: Penguin, 1976.

Lemke, Sieglinde. *Primitivist Modernism: Black Culture and the Origins of Transatlantic Modernism*. New York: Oxford University Press, 1998.

Lorsch, Susan E. *Where Nature Ends: Literary Responses to the Designification of Landscape*. Rutherford, N.J.: Fairleigh Dickinson University Press; London: Associated University Presses, 1983.

Lovejoy, Arthur O. *The Great Chain of Being*. Cambridge, Mass.: Harvard University Press, 1974.

Lyotard, Jean-Francois. *The Inhuman: Reflections on Time*. Trans. Geoffrey Bennington and Rachel Bowlby. Stanford, Calif.: Stanford University Press, 1991.

Mays, Benjamin E. *The Negro's God as Reflected in His Literature*. New York: Negro Universities Press, 1969.

McDowell, Deborah E. "Introduction." *Quicksand and Passing*. Ed. Deborah E. McDowell. New Brunswick, N.J.: Rutgers University Press, 1986. ix–xxxv.

Mensah, Emmanuel Kofi. "Thoughts From Africa's Leading Secular Humanist Activist." *African American Humanism: An Anthology*. Buffalo: Prometheus, 1991.

Miller, J. Hillis. *The Disappearance of God: Five Nineteenth-Century Writers*. Urbana: University of Illinois Press, 2000.

Mills, Charles W. *The Racial Contract*. Ithaca, N.Y.: Cornell University Press, 1997.

Morgan, Edmund. *Visible Saints: The History of a Puritan Idea*. New York: New York University Press, 1963.

Morrison, Toni. *Beloved*. New York: Penguin, 1988.

Nielsen, Kai. *Naturalism and Religion*. Amherst: Prometheus, 2001.

Nietzsche, Friedrich. *Anti-Christ*. Trans. R. J. Hollingdale. New York: Random House, 1989.

———. *The Case of Wagner. The Birth of Tragedy and The Case of Wagner*. Trans. Walter Kaufmann. New York: Vintage Books, 1967.

———. *The Gay Science*. Trans. Walter Kaufmann. New York: Penguin, 1990.

———. *On the Genealogy of Morals*. Trans. Walter Kaufmann and R. J. Hollingdale. New York: Random House, 1989.

———. *Twilight of the Idols*. Trans. R. J. Hollingdale. New York: Random House, 1989.

Pierce, Yolanda. *Hell Without Fires: Slavery, Christianity, and the Antebellum Spiritual Narrative*. Gainesville: University Press of Florida, 2005.

Pinn, Anthony B. *By These Hands: A Documentary History of African American Humanism*. New York: New York University Press, 2001.

———. *Varieties of African American Religious Experience*. Minneapolis: Fortress Press, 1998.

Proust, Marcel. *Swann's Way*. Trans. C. K. Scott Moncrieff. New York: Random House, 1970.

Raboteau, Albert J. *Canaan Land: A Religious History of African Americans*. New York: Oxford University Press, 2001.

Rampersad, Arnold. *The Life of Langston Hughes*. Vol. 1. New York: Oxford University Press, 1986.

Redding, J. Saunders. *On Being Negro in America*. Indianapolis: Charter Books, 1962.

Rorty, Richard. *Contingency, Irony, and Solidarity*. Cambridge, England: Cambridge University Press, 1989.

Russell, Bertrand. *Why I Am Not a Christian*. New York: Simon and Schuster, 1957.

Said, Edward. *Culture and Imperialism*. New York: Vintage Books, 1993.

———. *Humanism and Democratic Criticism*. New York: Columbia University Press, 2004.

———. *Orientalism*. New York: Vintage Books, 1979.

Sartre, Jean-Paul. "The Humanism of Existentialism." *Essays in Existentialism*. Secaucus, N.J.: Carol, 1999. 31–62.

Schiller, Friedrich. *On the Aesthetic Education of Man*. Trans. Reginald Snell. New York: Continuum, 1990.

Schwartz, Regina M. *The Curse of Cain: The Violent Legacy of Monotheism*. Chicago: University of Chicago Press, 1997.

Shakespeare, William. *As You Like It. Riverside Shakespeare*. Boston: Houghton Mifflin, 1974. 365–402.

Sheehan, Paul. *Modernism, Narrative, and Humanism*. Cambridge, England: Cambridge University Press, 2002.

Stephen, Leslie. *An Agnostic's Apology: Poisonous Opinions, in Selected Writings in British Intellectual History*. Chicago: University of Chicago Press, 1979.

Taylor, Clyde. "Black Writing as Immanent Humanism. *Southern Review* 21:3 (Summer 1985): 790–800.

Thrower, James. *Western Atheism: A Short History*. Amherst: Prometheus, 2000.

Tillich, Paul. *Dynamics of Faith*. New York: Harper and Row, 1957.

Toomer, Jean. "Kabnis." *Cane*. New York: W. W. Norton, 1988. 83–117.

Walker, Alice. *The Color Purple*. Orlando: Harcourt, 1982.

Wall, Cheryl A. *Women of the Harlem Renaissance*. Bloomington: Indiana University Press, 1995.

Whitman, Walt. *Song of Myself. Leaves of Grass and Selected Prose*. Toronto: Random House, 1981. 23–75.

Wilson, A. N. *God's Funeral*. New York: W. W. Norton, 1999.

Wood, Forrest G. *The Arrogance of Faith: Christianity and Race in America From the Colonial Era to the Twentieth Century*. Boston: Northeastern University Press, 1991.

Woolf, Virginia. "A Sketch of the Past." *Moments of Being*. New York: Harcourt Brace Jovanovich, 1978.

Wright, Richard. *Black Boy*. San Francisco: HarperPerennial Classics, 1993.

———. *The Outsider*. San Francisco: HarperPerennial Classics, 1993.

Index

Michael Lackey teaches at Wellesley College. A recipient of the Alexander von Humboldt Fellowship, he has published articles on Mark Twain, Gerard Manley Hopkins, Friedrich Nietzsche, Joseph Conrad, Virginia Woolf, Nella Larsen, Frantz Fanon, and Paul Celan.